# MODERN
# LANDSCAPE
# QUILTS

## 14 QUILT PROJECTS INSPIRED
## BY THE GREAT OUTDOORS

Donna McLeod

DAVID & CHARLES

www.davidandcharles.com

TO MATT AND OUR GIRLS—
MY HOME AND FAVORITE
TRAVEL COMPANIONS.

AND TO MA,
FOR LEAVING YOUR SEWING
MACHINE WITH ME.

# CONTENTS

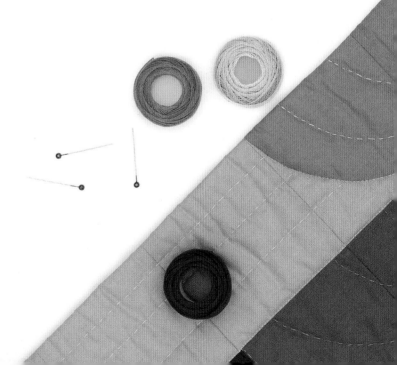

# INTRODUCTION

Writing this intro was hard, but what isn't hard are the projects in this book. As a self-taught quilter who appreciates approachable and easy-to-follow quilt patterns, I'm beyond thrilled to share these projects with you.

Whether you're new to the craft or a seasoned quilter, I wanted to offer a well-rounded collection of scenic designs. So, I went all out (and everywhere) to deliver you a variety of modern, versatile quilt patterns using basic quilt blocks.

Speaking of variety, I included an illustrative guide on how to finish your quilts by machine or by hand. If you're like me, there are days when I prefer to do a bit of slow stitching and other days when I want to do a quick weekend project. This book covers both cravings and ensures you have everything you need to complete your quilt from start to finish.

When I first began quilting, I was struck by the therapeutic joy of sewing fabrics together to create a usable work of art. It's a wonderfully tactile craft that's both stimulating and soothing; a part of my life where I can be carefree, and where I allow myself to embrace mistakes rather than overanalyze them. On top of their mental health benefits, quilts also have a built-in reputation of getting passed down from one generation to another. It's a delight to see my very first quilts being used every day by my kids to keep them warm, for comfort, and to build forts with. I simply cannot recommend it enough.

All of the designs in this book are inspired by the diverse physical regions and lands that belong to the Indigenous peoples of California. It's a place my family and I enjoy exploring and learning from. I hope you find a design here that satisfies your wanderlust, or that reminds you of your home or favorite outdoor adventure.

Most of all, I hope you enjoy these projects as much as I had fun bringing these designs to life.

## xo DONNA

## WHAT TO EXPECT

This book covers all the basics on how to make a quilt from start to finish, but it's important to distinguish piecing versus quilting. I'd love us to be on the same page, so let's briefly go over the difference between the two and what this book is about.

For simplicity, making a quilt from start to finish can be broken down into two main parts:

- **Part 1: PIECING**
- **Part 2: QUILTING**

### PIECING

The primary focus of this book is on piecing, the process of sewing fabrics together to make a quilt top. While there are various piecing techniques for sewing a quilt top, all of the projects in this book are traditionally pieced (also called patchwork piecing). This means two fabric pieces are facing each other so that when they are sewn together, the stitches are hidden on the back.

### QUILTING

Quilting is a broad term often used to describe piecing, but it's technically the process of stitching through the following layers that make a quilt:

- **The Quilt Top:** The projects in this book are all quilt tops, the layer that showcases the pattern's design. Huge attention seeker.
- **The Batting:** The middle inside layer that gives the quilt its squishy, cuddly body. Very private.
- **The Backing:** The underside of the quilt. Loves playing the supporting role forever.

While there are instructions for each step of the piecing and quilting processes, please don't expect this book to spend a lot of time on decorative stitches, color theory, or master machine- and hand-quilting. I won't leave you hanging, but I'm more interested in providing you with easy-to-digest projects using fresh, minimalist landscape designs.

# PLANNING + PIECING

As with most crafts, starting a project off on the right foot can eliminate a lot of potential issues down the road. In this section, we'll touch on preparation basics and review an important cutting note that steers away from the industry standard of cutting fabrics (**see Pressing + Cutting**).

There's also a **Tips + Troubleshooting** section which covers some helpful pointers for a smooth journey.

If your wanderlust is too strong to wait and you want to dive straight into making the quilts, be sure to review the **Projects** introduction, which includes relevant guidelines before you begin a project.

# TOOLS FOR PIECING

As someone who's thrown various hobbies to the wall pasta-style to see what sticks, I know all too well that investing in tools can be daunting. Aside from the sewing machine and the fabrics, the following are the recommended tools to piece the quilt tops in this book.

1  **45mm rotary cutter and replacement blades.** This standard sewing tool will make cutting your fabric as smooth as butter. Replace your blade when you find yourself exerting force to make cuts.

2  **24 x 36in self-healing cutting mat.** The standard size surface for cutting fabric.

3  **6½ x 24in acrylic ruler.** Great size for cutting your fabric.

4  **9½in square ruler.** The built-in diagonal line is suitable for trimming half square triangle (HST) blocks.

5  **6 x 12in rectangle ruler.** The ideal size for trimming the half rectangle triangle (HRT) blocks in this book.

6  **Iron and ironing board (not shown).** A long and sturdy ironing board is preferable for pressing long strips of fabric, but whatever you've got at home should do.

7  **Fabric marker.** I use a disappearing ink marker, but these come in different forms such as pencils, pens, and chalk. Test yours on a fabric scrap before use.

8  **Detail scissors.** A small pair is great for snipping threads and useful if you plan on hand quilting your project.

9  **Painter's tape.** This versatile tool will come in handy for labeling fabric pieces, basting a quilt, and using its edges as a guide to align fabrics on the sewing machine.

10  **Glass-headed sewing pins.** These keep your fabrics from shifting during sewing, and won't melt beneath the iron when pressing.

11  **Sewing machine needles.** The pencil of the sewing world. Have a few extras handy to replace your needles after about six hours of use or in case a needle breaks. Your sewing machine and fabrics are not fans of dull needles.

12  **Seam ripper.** The eraser of the sewing world. This little MVP (most valuable player!) can undo seam mistakes.

13  **Thread.** Higher number threads equal finer threads. A 50-weight cotton thread is the standard.

14  **Paper, cardstock, pencil, and paper scissors (not shown).** For projects that require templates in this book (**see Templates**). There's no need to buy cardstock. Cereal boxes, photo backings, rigid mailing envelopes, or anything sturdier than paper will do.

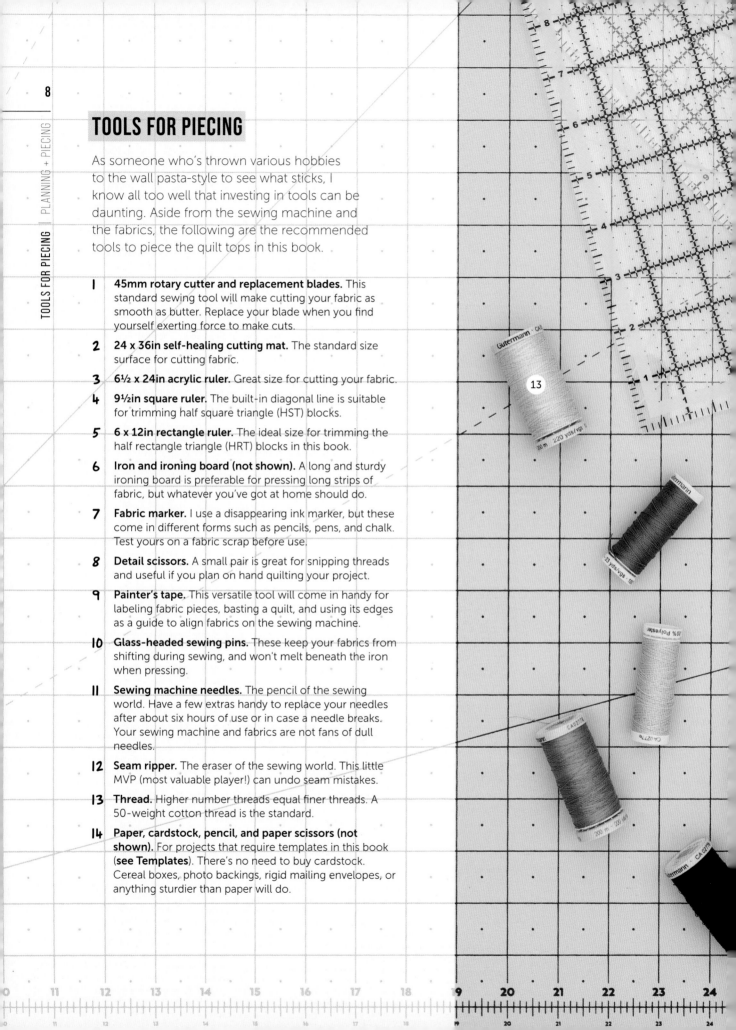

# UNDERSTANDING FABRICS

Let's talk about fabric. It's flexible, versatile, and is also what quilts are made with. Quilts can be made using various types of fabric, but projects in this book assume your fabrics are:

- quilting cotton (it's breathable, easy to work with, and readily available)
- 42in wide (with selvages removed)
- solid or non-directional fabrics

*PRINT DIRECTION: DIRECTIONAL PRINTED FABRICS NEED TO BE SEWN IN A CERTAIN DIRECTION. THE PROJECTS IN THIS BOOK ASSUME YOUR FABRICS ARE NON-DIRECTIONAL (SEE GLOSSARY).*

## FABRIC FEATURES

**Bias.** Woven fabric is composed of interlacing vertical (warp) and horizontal (weft) threads. The diagram shows the direction of the warp and weft threads and the fabric's stretchability. Fabric is extra stretchy when it's cut on the bias (diagonal), making it vulnerable to distortion. Keep this in mind when pressing and handling your cut pieces and blocks.

**Selvage.** The unusable finished edge of the fabric width that prevents the fabric from unraveling is called the selvage. The projects in this book refer to 42in usable width of fabric (WOF). That means selvages should be trimmed off before subcutting the WOF strips and, if applicable, before sewing your backing fabric pieces together.

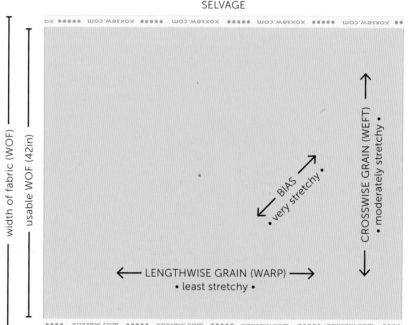

SELVAGE

width of fabric (WOF)

usable WOF (42in)

CROSSWISE GRAIN (WEFT)
• moderately stretchy •

BIAS
• very stretchy •

RAW EDGE

LENGTHWISE GRAIN (WARP)
• least stretchy •

SELVAGE

*SOME SELVAGE ENDS WILL INCLUDE INFORMATION SUCH AS THE MANUFACTURER AND THE FABRIC COLLECTION.*

## YARDAGE + PRECUTS

### FABRIC REQUIREMENTS

The yardage listed in each project (precut fabrics excluded) is calculated with at least 1in margin of error. Yardage with less than 1in of wiggle room was bumped up to the next ⅛yd increment.

### PRECUT DIMENSIONS

Precut fabrics come in a variety of shapes and sizes. Several projects in the book include an option to substitute yardage with two popular precut fabrics:

- Fat Quarter (FQ) measures 21 x 18in
- Fat Eighth (FE) measures 21 x 9in

Cutting instructions are based on yardage, so additional subcuts are likely required if using precut fabrics.

## WASHING FABRIC

Pre-washing is simply washing your fabrics before starting a project. I only have two rules when it comes to washing fabrics:

**1.** Never wash precut fabrics! Small pieces of fabric don't hold up well in a washing machine. (**Note:** The projects in this book assume precut fabrics are not washed.)

**2.** Use dye-trapping sheets if pre-washing fabrics (see below). Throw in one or two sheets for your finished quilt, too! These mighty absorbers help protect your fabrics/quilt from dye transfer or discoloration.

I find this topic to be a matter of personal preference, so here's a list of pros and cons to consider:

QUILT MADE USING NON PRE-WASHED FABRIC: FABRIC IS SMOOTH AND FLAT

THE SAME QUILT AFTER WASHING: FABRIC HAS SHRUNK AND GIVES THE QUILT A SOFT, CRINKLY LOOK

*Quilt pattern: This Way Home (xoxsew.com)*

### PRE-WASHING FABRIC:

Pros:

- Eliminates color bleeding
- Finished quilt post-wash will generally look the same with minimal shrinkage
- Removes manufacturing chemicals

Cons:

- You may need to purchase additional fabric if there's too much shrinkage
- Requires additional prep time (washing, drying, starching, ironing, trimming frayed edges)
- Water waste

### NOT PRE-WASHING FABRIC:

Pros:

- Eliminates additional prep time
- Easier to cut and sew
- Finished quilt will shrink after washing, giving it a soft, crinkly look and feel (although this could be a con for you!)

Cons:

- Finished quilt will shrink after washing
- Finished quilt will be more susceptible to fabric dye bleeding when washed.

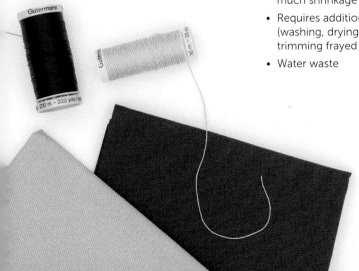

**TO WASH OR NOT:** I DON'T PRE-WASH TO AVOID THE EXTRA PREP AND IRONING TIME. PLUS, I LIVE IN DROUGHT-SUSCEPTIBLE CALIFORNIA, AND WAS RAISED TO ONLY DO LAUNDRY WHEN THE HAMPER IS FULL!

# CHOOSING COLORS

Sometimes, the most challenging – and exciting! – part of a project is starting it. With so many possibilities in the world of color, finding a combination that suits you can feel overwhelming. The color wheel is a great way to understand color relationships and can help you create your ideal color combination for your project. Here's a little overview to take into account as you plan your project.

## EXPERIMENTING WITH COLOR

Color not only affects the look of a quilt, but it often elicits an emotional response. Warm colors are stimulating and evoke strong emotions, while cool colors are linked with a sense of peace and tranquility. Using a combination of warm and cool colors or mixing colors of different values and saturation can take the visual interest of your quilt to the next level.

## BASIC COLOR COMBINATIONS

**Complementary.** Colors on opposite sides of the wheel; creates a high-contrast look.

**Analogous.** Neighboring colors; creates a coordinated, low-contrast look.

**Monochromatic.** Same color but with different variations in value (lightness) and/or saturation (intensity) for a minimal, clean look.

**Gradient.** Gradual transition from one color or another; creates a modern and colorful look.

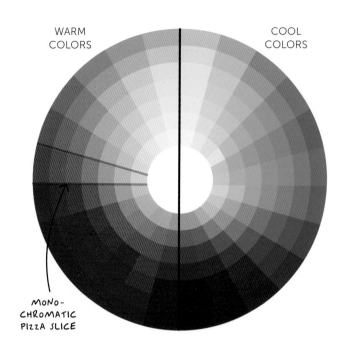

WARM COLORS · COOL COLORS

MONO-CHROMATIC PIZZA SLICE

## COLOR CARDS

A fabric color card showcases the available solid colors that a manufacturer carries, and are my favorite tools to explore and find colors for my next quilt project, especially since my choices will be limited to fabric availability. In addition, digital swatches may be more expansive, but color cards provide an accurate representation of a fabric's color and texture, making it an ideal resource for those who shop online.

I tend to cut my cards into individual swatches, then glue them to a magnet-backed piece of cardboard to keep them organized. The individual swatches allow me to view color combinations with ease.

COLOR CARDS ARE NOT AN ESSENTIAL TOOL TO BEGIN A PROJECT, BUT IF YOU INTEND TO MAKE A LOT OF QUILTS, IT'S A WORTHWHILE INVESTMENT TO HAVE IN YOUR ARSENAL.

COMPLEMENTARY   ANALOGOUS   MONOCHROMATIC

SIMPLE MONOCHROMATIC LANDSCAPE

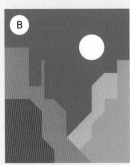

DARK, COOL TONED SKY

LIGHT, COOL TONED SKY

TRANSITION COLORS

NEUTRAL COLORED SKY

## CREATING DEPTH

The landscape designs in this book provide a great exercise for creating depth, by mixing colors and adjusting color variations. Dark, vivid colors are typically used for closer objects, and gradually get lighter and less intense as objects recede into the distance. For landscapes, starting with a monochromatic color scheme can be a helpful shortcut to achieve the illusion of depth. Simply take a (ridiculously thin) pizza slice from the color wheel and allow it to do most of the work.

To demonstrate, I'll grab the orange pizza slice from the color wheel and apply it to the Canyon design, from darkest (closest object) to lightest (sky). Notice how the different variations of the same color create a distinct foreground and background **(A)**.

### COOL IT DOWN

If I want to dial down the warmth, I can take a color from the opposite side of the color wheel to cool the sky **(B)**.

### VARY THE INTENSITY

Though I added a contrasting color, the sense of distance is somewhat lost because the blue has a similar intensity as the foreground. How about a lighter, less intense blue? **(C)**

### TRANSITION TONES

Now, if I want to cool the temperature further, I can swap out the warm distant canyons with cooler colors. I'll choose some blues that will transition nicely to the sky color **(D)**.

### MOVE INTO NEUTRAL

Hmm, how about I swap the sky with a more neutral color to bring in additional balance? Let's see if a light grey would work **(E)**.

### DON'T TAKE MY WORD FOR IT!

I could continue making adjustments, but the best way to learn about color is to play with it yourself! It can change the dynamic of a landscape and allow you to discover color combinations that you don't normally gravitate towards. The more you experiment, the better understanding you'll have of color relationships.

This brief exercise was a quick way to get your feet wet regarding depth and is, by no means, a set of rules. Also, don't let the landscape theme limit your color scheme. Pair a fuchsia sun with a turquoise tree – Roy G. Biv would approve.

## BEHIND THE SCENES

THOUGH I'M NOT A COLOR EXPERT, IT WAS A DELIGHT TO PLAY WITH DIFFERENT COLORS AND FABRICS, WHILE TRYING TO KEEP A COHESIVE PALETTE FOR THE PROJECTS IN THIS BOOK. REMEMBER TO HAVE FUN EXPERIMENTING!

# PRESSING + CUTTING

Get comfortable with your iron and rotary cutter – there's a lot of cutting and pressing in quilts. This chapter covers important notes that impact your quilt adventure so resist the urge to skip it!

## PRESSING YOUR FABRIC

Truth be told, pressing is one of my least favorite parts of sewing, but it's important to remove wrinkles and unwanted folds before cutting your fabric to achieve accurate cuts. Keep in mind that pressing is different to ironing. Ironing is a left-and-right motion; pressing is a lift-and-drop move. It's a less intrusive process that prevents fabric distortion.

You may decide to use starch to stabilize and stiffen fabrics beforehand, making it easier to cut and sew (especially useful for stretchy bias edges). I personally don't – again not a fan of extra prep time, especially if it involves an iron!

### PRESSING DIRECTION

There are two directions in which to press your seams:

**Pressing seams open.** Creates flatter seams and tends to result in more accurately-pieced blocks. However, the stitches will be more vulnerable to unraveling because the seams are exposed **(A)**.

**Pressing to one side.** Tends to be faster and it can be easier to match and nest your seams, but it can add undesirable bulk to your quilt **(B)**.

Instructions in this book will indicate when to press, but unless specifically stated, the direction is up to you. Whatever you decide, press your seams with care.

When sewing basic blocks, be sure to keep your pressing direction consistent to achieve more accurate piecing.

## CUTTING WITH ACCURACY

Cutting your fabric pieces accurately is crucial for precise piecing as it can prevent a lot of common issues down the road.

---

### IMPORTANT!

The dimensions in the cutting requirements are **width x height** from *your* perspective. Fabric pieces will be rotated during cutting, so the dimensions are based on how it's positioned in front of you. That means the width is always your first cut:

$$W \quad \times \quad H$$

(MEASURE LEFT TO RIGHT)   (MEASURE TOP TO BOTTOM)

This is important to note because it contradicts the industry's standard for subcutting WOF strips, where the strip height is often listed first.

---

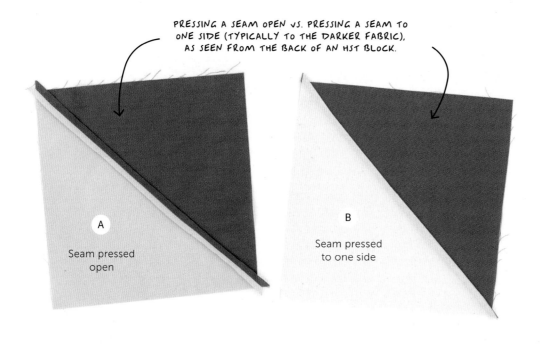

PRESSING A SEAM OPEN VS. PRESSING A SEAM TO ONE SIDE (TYPICALLY TO THE DARKER FABRIC), AS SEEN FROM THE BACK OF AN HST BLOCK.

A
Seam pressed open

B
Seam pressed to one side

## HOW TO CUT YOUR FABRIC

Let's do a quick review on how to square up your fabrics and cut them in to pieces. All diagrams are based on a right-handed perspective.

Here is an example of the cutting instructions you'll find in the projects, and how to prepare and cut your fabric.

**Cut 1 piece** 5in x WOF
**Subcut:**
**(2)** 5in squares
**(1)** 2½ x 4in (width x height)

### SQUARING UP

**1.** With selvage ends together, line up the folded edge of your fabric along one of the horizontal lines of the cutting mat.

**2.** Use the edge of a ruler to trim off the uneven edge **(A)**. Now your fabric is ready to be cut into pieces!

### CUTTING A STRIP

**3.** Continuing from the previous step, carefully rotate your fabric 180-degrees so the newly trimmed straight edge is lined up along the 0in vertical line of the cutting mat. Use the ruler marks or your cutting mat guidelines to cut 1 piece 5in x WOF, as shown on the diagram **(B)**.

**4.** Unfold the strip and turn it 90-degrees. Trim off the selvage ends.

### MAKING SUBCUTS

**5.** Now it's time to make the subcuts. First, cut (2) 5in squares.

**6.** For the (1) 2½ x 4in piece, cut a 2½in width from the remaining WOF strip. Then trim the height to 4in **(C )**. Note how the first number of the dimension is always the width of the fabric from *your* point of view.

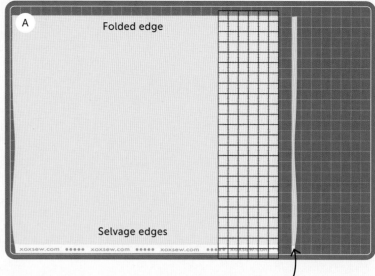

Folded edge

Selvage edges

Discard unusable piece

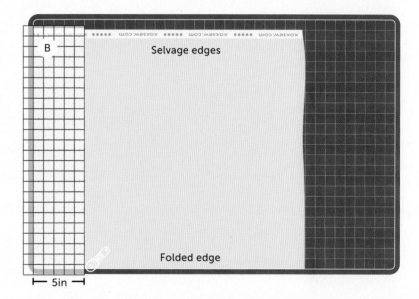

B

Selvage edges

Folded edge

⊢ 5in ⊣

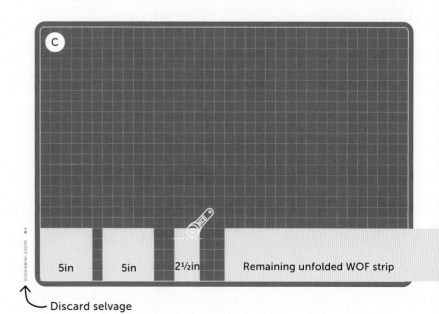

C

xoxsew.com

5in    5in    2½in    Remaining unfolded WOF strip

Discard selvage

# BASIC BLOCKS

Most of the projects in this book will use one or more basic blocks, which are compiled in this chapter for easy reference. There are also instructions on how to sew with a scant ¼in seam allowance – the optimal way to achieve accurate blocks.

Before diving in, my favorite piece of advice is to use some scraps to make a test block. It sounds like a waste of time and materials, but it's quite the opposite: I once used three yards of fabric incorrectly, not knowing that I'd sewn and trimmed them inaccurately until the last moment.

So, on that cheerful note, **see Tips + Troubleshooting** for more helpful pointers to complete your project!

FOR MY FELLOW LEFT-HANDED QUILTERS: THE DIAGRAMS ARE BASED ON A RIGHT-HANDED PERSPECTIVE.

**OI  STRIPS**
LANDSCAPES: Coastal / Meadow / Woodland

**02  HALF SQUARE TRIANGLES (HSTs)**
LANDSCAPES: Lake / Canyon / Mountain / Meadow

**03  HALF RECTANGLE TRIANGLES (HRTs)**
LANDSCAPE: Mountain

**04  QUARTER CIRCLES**
LANDSCAPES: Canyon / Coastal / Woodland

## KEY

———————  marked line

————  trim size

- - - - - - -  sewing line

- - - - - - -  cut line

**RST**  right sides together

**HST**  half square triangle

**HRT**  half rectangle triangle

**WOF**  width of fabric (42in)

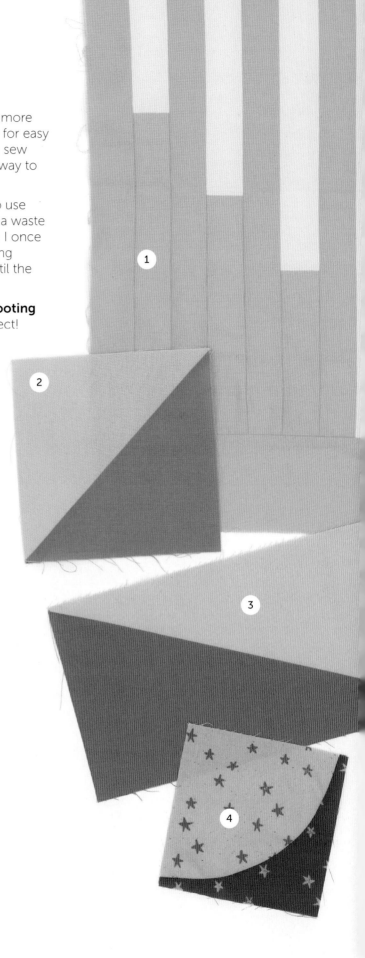

## SCANT ¼IN SEAM

A ¼in seam allowance is the standard measurement quilters use to sew two pieces of fabric together, indicated by the black dashed line **(A)**.

However, a common quilting issue is sewing a block that ends up too small because some of the fabric is lost in the fold of the pressed seam.

Using a scant ¼in seam allowance, indicated by the red dashed line **(A)** is a popular solution. It is a thread width or two narrower than a ¼in, compensating for the fabric lost to the fold.

### SETTING A SCANT ¼IN SEAM

Finding your scant ¼in seam without the use of fancy tools requires good ol' trial and error. First, figure out the width of your current seam allowance:

**1.** Cut (3) fabric scraps measuring 2½ x 5in **(B)**.

**2.** Sew the fabrics together along the long side to create a block measuring 6½ x 5in **(C)**.

**3.** Press your seams open or to the side **(see Pressing + Cutting)**.

The middle block should now measure 2in wide. If that's what you have, then you're all set! If not, read on...

If the middle block is *less* than 2in, then it's time to find that scant seam by proceeding to Step 4.

**4.** If your sewing machine's needle plate allows you to move the needle to the right, adjust your needle position a thread width to the right.

If your needle doesn't move to the side, position your fabrics a thread width to the left when sewing your seams. To ensure consistency, use painter's tape to mark the line where your fabric edge will sit **(D) (E)**.

**5.** Repeat steps 1–4 as needed, sewing the fabrics together with the adjusted needle or tape position until the middle block measures 2in.

Once you find your scant ¼in seam allowance, try to stay consistent when sewing and pressing your quilt blocks to maintain accuracy.

**Note:** Remember to revert back to a ¼in seam allowance when assembling your quilt top. Personally, I find myself sewing with a scant ¼in seam almost exclusively. Once again, this will be a matter of preference and/or comfort level.

---

**DELICATE FABRICS:** THE ONLY TIME I WOULD HESITATE TO USE A SCANT ¼IN SEAM ALLOWANCE ARE ON FABRICS THAT ARE PRONE TO UNRAVELING, SUCH AS LINEN. USE A SHORTER STITCH LENGTH (SUCH AS 1.8MM) TO REINFORCE YOUR SEAMS.

---

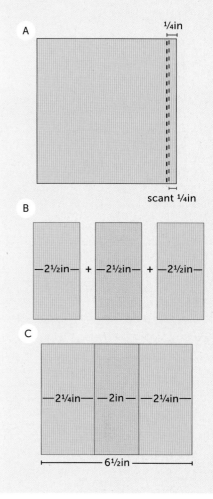

A

¼in

scant ¼in

B

—2½in— + —2½in— + —2½in—

C

—2¼in— —2in— —2¼in—

6½in

D

PLACE THE TAPE EDGE A THREAD WIDTH TO THE LEFT, TOWARDS THE NEEDLE.

SOME FABRIC IS LOST TO THE FOLD AFTER SEAMS ARE PRESSED!

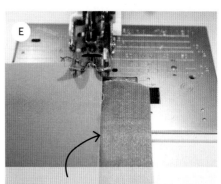

E

ALIGN YOUR FABRIC EDGES WITH THIS WHEN SEWING.

## STRIPS

The instructions given in the projects for creating strips are straightforward, but here are some tips to ensure accurate results.

### TIPS FOR SEWING STRIPS

**Use pins.** To keep fabric edges aligned and prevent the fabrics from shifting as you sew, use pins along the whole length of the strip **(A)**.

**Scant ¼in seam.** A scant ¼in seam allowance is recommended for sewing narrow fabric strips together. It helps prevent the common issue of smaller-than-expected blocks **(B)**.

**Alternate directions.** Prevent your strips from bowing by alternating the feed direction through your sewing machine **(C)**.

**Press seams.** Regardless of your pressing direction preference, finger press your seams prior to pressing with a hot iron to prevent strips from bowing.

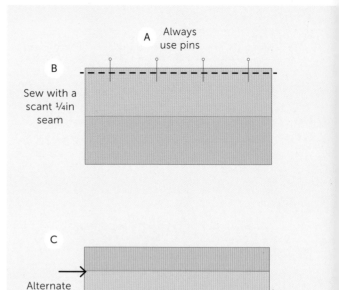

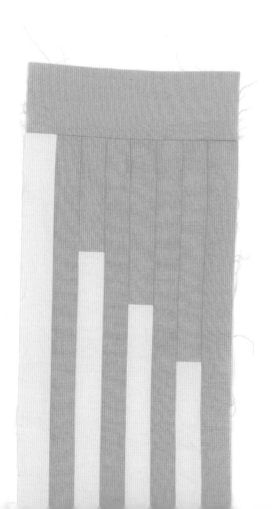

## STRIP PIECING

Strip piecing is a method used for the Meadow projects, where long strips of fabric that are sewn together into units are cut into smaller blocks. It is a time-saving technique, but it typically results in leftover scraps. Save the leftovers for a future project!

For the strip piecing method, adjust your sewing machine to a smaller stitch length (such as 1.8mm) to reinforce your seams and prevent the ends from unraveling.

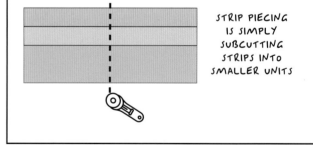

STRIP PIECING IS SIMPLY SUBCUTTING STRIPS INTO SMALLER UNITS

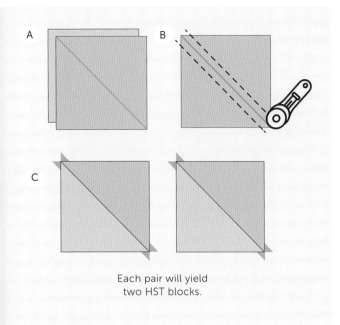

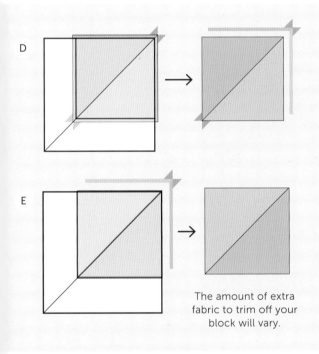

Each pair will yield
two HST blocks.

The amount of extra
fabric to trim off your
block will vary.

## HALF SQUARE TRIANGLES (HSTs)

There are several ways to create HSTs, but all the projects in this book use the popular two-at-a-time method. As a result, you may yield more HSTs than the pattern requires.

### SEWING

**1.** Continuing from the project you're working with, mark a diagonal line on the wrong side of one square from a pair. Place the squares RST with the marked square on top **(A)**.

**2.** Sew a scant ¼in seam on both sides of the diagonal line. Then, cut along the diagonal line **(B)**.

**3.** Repeat previous steps for the remaining pairs. Before proceeding to the next step, refer to your project to ensure you can discard extra HST blocks (there's no need to press and trim blocks that you don't need for the project!) **(C)**.

**4.** Press the blocks.

---

CHAIN PIECING: REFER TO THE TIPS +
TROUBLESHOOTING SECTION TO SEW YOUR
HST BLOCKS MORE EFFICIENTLY.

---

### TRIMMING

A square ruler that is larger than the block is recommended. For blocks larger than your ruler, use the 45-degree diagonal line on your cutting mat instead as a guide to line up and trim your HSTs.

**1.** Align the 45-degree line of the ruler to the diagonal seam and allow extra fabric outside the trim size (indicated in red) **(D)**. Trim the two exposed edges.

**2.** Rotate the fabric 180-degrees. Align the 45-degree line of the ruler to the diagonal seam, ensuring the newly trimmed edges are aligned to the trim size (indicated in red). Trim the exposed edges **(E)**.

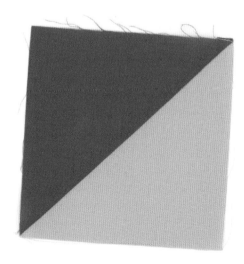

## HALF RECTANGLE TRIANGLES (HRTs)

The Mountain projects use two types of HRTs. For simplicity, we'll refer to them as west HRTs and east HRTs to reflect which side of the mountain they will be placed when assembling the quilt top.

**Note:** Make sure that you work with one type of HRT at a time as they can get easily mixed up, especially when working with solid fabrics!

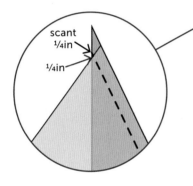

In both directions, east and west, the fabric intersects at ¼in, but remember to sew a scant ¼in seam. The untrimmed block will look a little wonky, but don't be alarmed – the corners will be trimmed off.

### SEWING

Place one pair of triangles, RST. Offset the edges by a ¼in so the pointy tip of each triangle is sticking out and the fabrics intersect at ¼in as shown. Pin and sew a scant ¼in seam along the diagonal side. Press. Repeat with the remaining pairs.

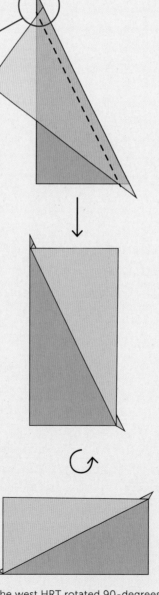

WEST HRT

The west HRT rotated 90-degrees counter clockwise

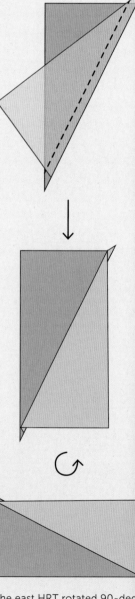

EAST HRT

The east HRT rotated 90-deg[rees] counter clockwise

## TRIMMING THE WEST HRT

**Trim all HRT blocks to 10½ x 5½in** as indicated by the red rectangle in the following diagrams. For this example, we are trimming a west HRT.

**1.** On your ruler, mark a dot ¼in inward from the corners of the trim size where the diagonal seam will run **(A)**.

**2.** Set your ruler on top of a west HRT, aligning the diagonal seam with the ¼in ruler marks. Allow extra fabric beyond the trim size. Trim along the exposed edges **(B)**.

**3.** Rotate the block 180-degrees. Set your ruler on top, aligning the diagonal seam on the ¼in ruler marks and the newly trimmed edges along the trim size. Trim the exposed edges **(C)**.

**4.** Repeat steps 2–3 for the remaining west HRTs.

---

**TRUST THE PROCESS:** YOUR RULER WILL LOOK SKEWED IN RELATION TO THE BLOCK DURING TRIMMING.

---

## TRIMMING THE EAST HRT

Follow the trimming instructions for the west HRTs, steps 1–4, for the east HRTs. However, ensure you create new ¼in ruler marks in step 1, as the diagonal seam will run the opposite direction **(D)** .

## BLOCK POINTS

Remember that sharp points are cut off to ensure a perfect HRT during quilt top assembly!

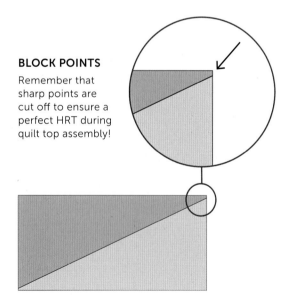

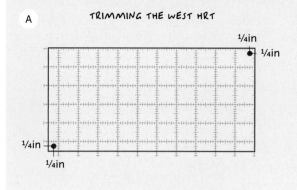

A · TRIMMING THE WEST HRT

¼in
¼in
¼in
¼in

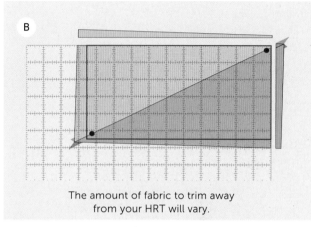

B

The amount of fabric to trim away from your HRT will vary.

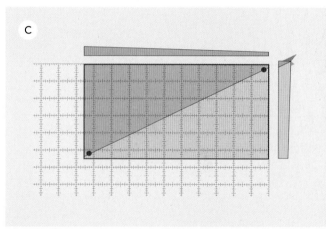

C

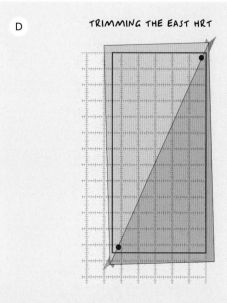

D · TRIMMING THE EAST HRT

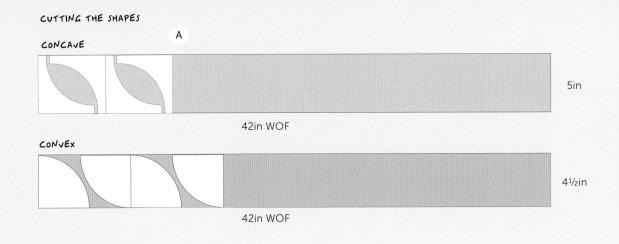

CUTTING THE SHAPES

CONCAVE

A

5in

42in WOF

CONVEX

4½in

42in WOF

# QUARTER CIRCLES

Sewing with curves can be intimidating, but
it's a fun break from sewing straight lines!
I've started with a few tips to help you cut
and sew the smoothest quarter circles.

### MAKING TEMPLATES

Starting off your project with accurately cut pieces is
important, so take care when creating the convex and
concave templates for quarter circles (see Templates).

### CUTTING THE SHAPES

To minimize fabric waste, use your templates to cut the
convex and concave pieces as shown (A). Take your time
and handle the fabric with care.

Although a standard 45mm rotary cutter will do the job,
consider using a smaller blade, such as 28mm. The size
is more maneuverable when cutting curves, resulting in
greater accuracy when cutting and piecing.

### SEWING

**1.** Fold a convex piece and its corresponding concave
piece in half to create a center mark. Fold each end to the
center mark to create two diagonal marks (B).

**2.** With RST, place the concave piece on top of the convex
piece. Match the center creases and pin together. Repeat
with the remaining diagonal marks and the fabric ends (C).

**3.** Sew a scant ¼in seam slowly along the curve, removing
the pins as you sew and pivoting as needed to avoid
accidentally sewing a pleat. Finger press the seams (D).

**4.** Repeat Steps 1–3 for the remaining convex and
concave pairs. Press.

---

**STITCH LENGTH:** ADJUST YOUR SEWING MACHINE
TO A SMALLER STITCH LENGTH (SUCH AS 1.8MM)
TO CREATE A SMOOTH, CURVED SEAM AND
PREVENT THE ENDS FROM UNRAVELING.

---

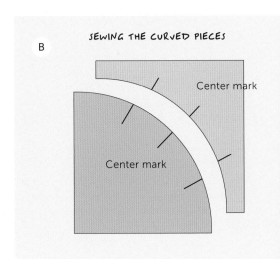

SEWING THE CURVED PIECES

B

Center mark

Center mark

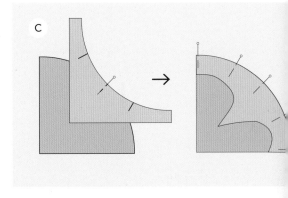

C

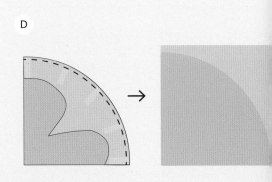

D

## TRIMMING THE BLOCK

E

¼in

¼in

The amount of fabric to trim away from your block will vary.

F

¼in

¼in

## TRIMMING THE BLOCK

The **trim size is 4½in** as indicated by the red square in the diagrams.

**1.** Set your ruler on top of the block, ensuring a ¼in seam allowance on the corners where the fabrics meet. Allow extra fabric beyond the trim size. Trim the exposed edges **(E)**.

**2.** Rotate the block 180-degrees. Set your ruler on top of the block so the newly trimmed edges are aligned to the trim size. Trim the exposed edges **(F)**.

LEVEL UP ON PINS: FEEL FREE TO USE MORE PINS TO SUIT YOUR COMFORT LEVEL. MORE PINS CAN YIELD A MORE ACCURATE BLOCK AND REQUIRES LESS MANEUVERING WHEN SEWING THE TWO PIECES TOGETHER.

# TIPS + TROUBLESHOOTING

Going with the flow on road trips is fun, but preparation is the key to a pleasant quilt journey. Fabric is easily stretched and pieced blocks can come out looking wonkier than desired. The thread weight, type of quilting cotton, and consistency of stitches can also affect the outcome. For me, the natural beauty of imperfections on a handmade quilt is what makes this such a wonderful craft. If your completed quilt top isn't flawless, be kind to yourself and take a moment to appreciate what you've made. Let's go over a few tips and tricks to take with you on the road.

### STRENGTHEN YOUR SEAMS

Some seams may come undone after trimming your blocks, or when strip piecing. To reinforce your seams without sewing over them again, one solution is to adjust the stitch length on your sewing machine. The standard stitch length is about 2.5, but shortening this (I recommend 1.8) will result in tighter seams that are less susceptible to unraveling **(A)**. The shorter stitches also create fewer angles, making this setting ideal for sewing curves. However, bear in mind that the more stitches there are on a seam, the more challenging it will be if you have to undo them.

Backstitching at the start and end of a seam also helps to secure stitches and prevent seams from unraveling. It's instructed during quilt top assembly, but you may find it useful for making basic blocks, too!

### CHAIN PIECING

Sewing blocks one directly after another in a long chain, without cutting the thread, is a technique called chain piecing **(B)**. This assembly-line style method is an efficient technique for making sets of blocks in one sitting. Once you've completed sewing a set of blocks, you simply snip the chain that connects them together **(C)**.

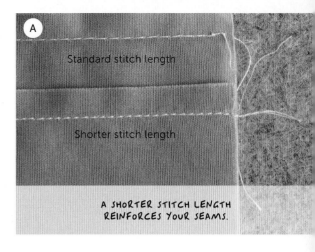

Standard stitch length

Shorter stitch length

A SHORTER STITCH LENGTH REINFORCES YOUR SEAMS.

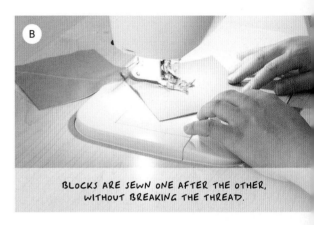

BLOCKS ARE SEWN ONE AFTER THE OTHER, WITHOUT BREAKING THE THREAD.

SNIP THE "CHAIN" THAT CONNECTS THE SET OF BLOCKS.

## MAKE A TEST BLOCK

I know, I know. It's easy to forgo this extra step. But if you want to avoid potential issues (and your seam ripper!) as much as possible, make a test block before diving into a quilt project.

Practice on leftover scraps, or have extra fabric on hand – you don't want to run out of the actual fabrics to be used for the project. It's possible you may need to adjust your seam allowance **(see Basic Blocks)** or it may lead you to discover an effective workflow to tackle your project.

A RULER GRIP CAN KEEP YOUR RULER STABLE, RESULTING IN MORE ACCURATE CUTTING.

## CUTTING ACCURATELY

While it might be tempting to jump into a project with both feet, it's important to get the preparations right. If your fabrics and templates aren't cut accurately, the outcome is unlikely to be accurate. Make sure your rotary cutter blade is sharp, and take your time when cutting. If your ruler keeps slipping, there are specialty tools such as a ruler grip or grip tape, to help keep it in place (**D**).

### SCANT ¼IN SEAM

A scant ¼in seam allowance (**see Basic Blocks**) is slightly narrower than ¼in. This is to resolve the fabric loss when seams are pressed, especially if pressed to one side. A scant ¼in seam allowance is recommended to make the blocks in this book, but you may also find it effective when assembling the quilt top.

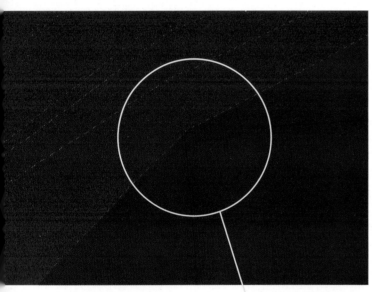

## RETAINING POINTS + CORNERS

To align blocks more accurately and be sure that the pointed tip of a block doesn't get sewn over, I use my fingernail to mark a crease where seams will be joined – this allows me to check where my stitches should go. This tip may bypass the seam allowance, but it can be a shortcut to patching up any discrepancies of an inaccurately-pieced block.

With right sides together, match up the fingernail crease marks and take a peek to get a preview of how the blocks will look when sewn (**E**). When you're satisfied, pin your blocks in place, then sew your pieces together (**F**).

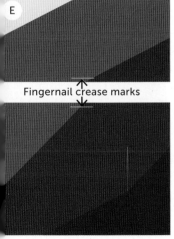
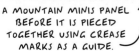

Fingernail crease marks

A MOUNTAIN MINIS PANEL BEFORE IT IS PIECED TOGETHER USING CREASE MARKS AS A GUIDE.

A MOUNTAIN MINIS PANEL WHEN PIECED TOGETHER.

# PROJECTS

Adventure awaits! But first, be sure to read the instructions and review the diagrams before cutting your fabrics. Here's a quick rundown of important information you'll need for the journey.

### FABRIC REQUIREMENTS

- Projects assume non-directional fabrics, and usable WOF with selvages removed is 42in. Yardage is calculated to allow some wiggle room for error. Additional subcuts may be required if using precut fabrics (**see Understanding Fabrics**).
- Backing fabric is calculated with some overage (**see Quilt Sandwich**).
- Binding fabric is based on 2½in strips (**see Finishing a Quilt**).

### CUTTING AND SEWING INSTRUCTIONS

- Dimensions are written as width x height from your perspective (**see Pressing + Cutting**).
- Cut fabric in the order listed to maximize yardage. As a result, some pieces may appear in different subcuts.
- Label your pieces! Instructions refer to labels rather than dimensions when piecing together.
- Seam allowance is ¼in, but a scant ¼in seam allowance is recommended to make the basic blocks (**see Basic Blocks**).
- Instructions will indicate when to press. In which direction, unless noted, is up to you (**see Pressing + Cutting**).

# LAKE

We're starting the adventure at the lake to get comfortable with HSTs, perhaps the most popular basic block in the quilting world. Large pieces make up the bulk of this landscape, allowing a wonderful exercise in working with blocks, big and small, while making sure the biggest project in this book is also easy to assemble.

## FINISHED SIZE
80 x 88in

---

## FABRIC REQUIREMENTS

| Fabric | Quantity |
|---|---|
| A | 1¾yds |
| B | 1½yds |
| C | ½yd |
| D | ¾yd |
| E | 1yd |
| F | ⅝yd |
| G | 1½yds |
| Backing | 7⅜yds |
| Binding | ¾yd |

---

## BASIC BLOCK
Half square triangles (HSTs)

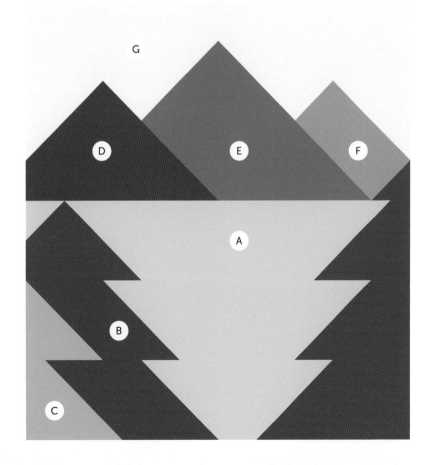

## CUTTING INSTRUCTIONS

- **See Projects** for important notes before you begin.
- Skipped labels (e.g. E2) are intentional.

**BACKING FABRIC**
**Cut 3 pieces** 88½in x WOF

**BINDING FABRIC**
**Cut 9 pieces** 2½in x WOF

## FABRIC A

**Cut 2 pieces** 17in x WOF
**Subcut:**
(3) 17in squares **A1**
(1) 24½ x 16½in **A4**

**Cut 1 piece** 16½in x WOF
**Subcut:**
(1) 36½ x 16½in **A3**

**Cut 1 piece** 9in x WOF
**Subcut:**
(1) 9in square **A2**
(1) 16½ x 8½in **A5**

## FABRIC B

**Cut 2 pieces** 17in x WOF
**Subcut:**
(4) 17in squares **B1**
(2) 4½ x 16½in **B6**

**Cut 1 piece** 17½in x WOF
**Subcut:** see cutting diagram for clarity
(1) 16½in square **B3**
(2) 9in squares **B2**
(1) 16½ x 8½in **B5**
(1) 8½in square **B4**

## FABRIC C

**Cut 1 piece** 17in x WOF
**Subcut:**
(1) 17in square **C1**
(1) 4½ x 16½in **C6**

## FABRIC D

**Cut 1 piece** 17in x WOF
**Subcut:**
(1) 17in square **D1**
(1) 16½in square **D3**
(1) 8½in square **D4**

**Cut 1 piece** 9in x WOF
**Subcut:**
(2) 9in squares **D2**

## FABRIC E

**Cut 2 pieces** 17in x WOF
**Subcut:**
(3) 17in squares **E1**
(1) 16½in square **E3**

## FABRIC F

**Cut 1 piece** 18in x WOF
**Subcut:** see cutting diagram for clarity
(1) 17in square **F1**
(3) 9in squares **F2**

## FABRIC G

**Cut 1 piece** 17in x WOF
**Subcut:**
(1) 17in square **G1**
(2) 24½ x 8½in **G3**

**Cut 1 piece** 9in x WOF
**Subcut:**
(4) 9in squares **G2**

**Cut 1 piece** 8½in x WOF
**Subcut:**
(2) 8½in squares **G4**

**Cut 2 pieces** 8½in x WOF **G5**

**FABRIC B: CUTTING DIAGRAM**

B1 | B1 | B6
B1 | B1 | B6
17½in — B3 | B2 | B2 | B5 | B4

42in WOF

**FABRIC F: CUTTING DIAGRAM**

18in — F1 | F2 | F2 | F2

42in WOF

## HST CONSTRUCTION

If the total HSTs required is an odd number, there will be an extra HST block. Discard or save any extra blocks for a future project!*

**1.** Pair the following A1-G1 pieces, RST. Refer to HST block instructions **(see Basic Blocks)** to sew and **trim each large HST block to 16½in.**

**2.** Pair the following A2, B2, D2, F2, and G2 pieces, RST. Refer to HST block instructions to sew and **trim each small HST block to 8½in.**

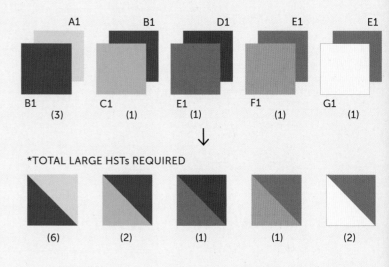

LARGE HST CONSTRUCTION

| A1 | B1 | D1 | E1 | E1 |
| B1 | C1 | E1 | F1 | G1 |
| (3) | (1) | (1) | (1) | (1) |

↓

*TOTAL LARGE HSTs REQUIRED

(6)   (2)   (1)   (1)   (2)

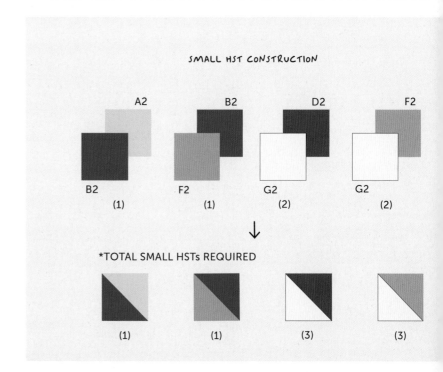

SMALL HST CONSTRUCTION

| A2 | B2 | D2 | F2 |
| B2 | F2 | G2 | G2 |
| (1) | (1) | (2) | (2) |

↓

*TOTAL SMALL HSTs REQUIRED

(1)   (1)   (3)   (3)

### BEHIND THE SCENES

LAKE AND LAKE MINI ARE THE ONLY PROJECTS THAT USE LARGE BASIC BLOCKS. THE SIZE MAY SAVE SOME TIME, BUT THEY CAN ALSO BE A BIT CUMBERSOME TO CUT, SEW, AND TRIM. THAT'S WHY YOU MIGHT NOTICE THE BASIC BLOCKS FOR THE REMAINING LANDSCAPE DESIGNS ARE MORE RULER-FRIENDLY!

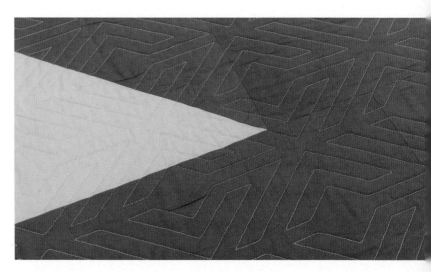

ASSEMBLY DIAGRAM

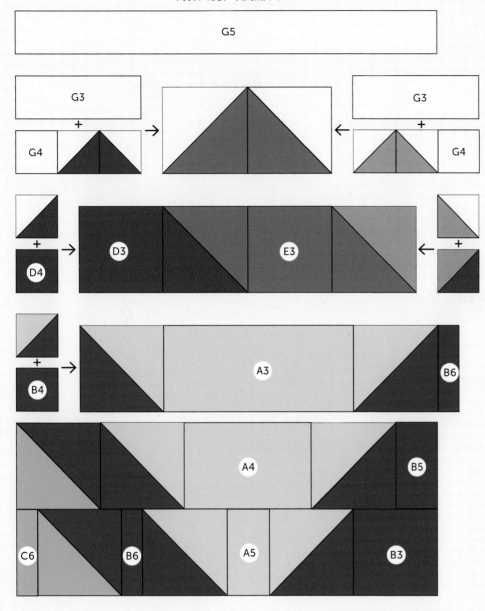

## QUILT TOP ASSEMBLY

**1.** Sew the (2) G5 pieces along the short edge, RST. Press seams open. **Trim to 80½in.**

**2.** Arrange the blocks as shown in the Assembly Diagram. Ensure HSTs are properly oriented.

**3.** First, sew the smaller pieces as indicated in the Assembly Diagram. Press. Then, sew the blocks into rows. Press.

**4.** Sew the rows together, pinning at each seam to keep the blocks and rows aligned. Backstitch at the start and end of each row to reinforce the seams. Press seams open.

See **Quilting + Finishing** to complete your project.

# LAKE MINI

Half the size of its bigger counterpart – and with fewer HSTs to manage – the Lake Mini may also be the fastest project to make in this book. Plus, you can use the large HST block leftovers to whip up a coordinating 16in square pillow cover!

## FINISHED SIZE
40 x 48in

———

## FABRIC REQUIREMENTS

| Fabric | Quantity |
| --- | --- |
| A | 1¼yds |
| B | 1yd |
| C | ½yd |
| Backing | 2¾yds |
| Binding | ⅜yd |

———

## BASIC BLOCK
Half square triangles (HSTs)

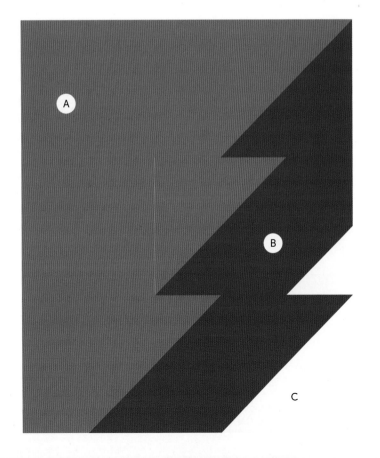

## CUTTING INSTRUCTIONS

- **See Projects** for important notes before you begin.

**BACKING FABRIC**
**Cut 2 pieces** 48in x WOF

**BINDING FABRIC**
**Cut 5 pieces** 2½in x WOF

## FABRIC A

**Cut 1 piece** 17in x WOF
**Subcut:**
(2) 17in squares **A1**
**Cut 1 piece** 16½in x WOF
**Subcut:**
(1) 24 ½ x 16½in **A2**
(1) 16½in square **A3**
**Cut 1 piece** 8½in x WOF
**Subcut:**
(1) 16½ x 8½in **A4**

## FABRIC B

**Cut 2 pieces** 17in x WOF
**Subcut:**
(3) 17in squares **B1**
(1) 9in square **B2**
(1) 8½in square **B3**

## FABRIC C

**Cut 1 piece** 17in x WOF
**Subcut:**
(1) 17in square **C1**
(1) 9in square **C2**

### HST CONSTRUCTION

#### Large HSTs

A1    B1

B1    C1

(2)    (1)

↓

#### *TOTAL HSTs REQUIRED

(3)    (1)

## HST CONSTRUCTION

There will be an extra block from each set of HSTs. Discard or save for a future project!*

**1.** Pair the following A1-C1 pieces, RST. Refer to HST block instructions **(see Basic Blocks)** to sew and **trim the total HSTs required to 16½in.**

**2.** Pair the B2 and C2 pieces, RST. Refer to HST block instructions to sew and **trim one small HST block to 8½in.**

## QUILT TOP ASSEMBLY

**1.** Arrange the blocks as shown in the Assembly Diagram.

**2.** Sew the small HST and B3 piece together as shown in the Assembly Diagram. Press.

**3.** Sew the blocks to form a row. Press. Repeat with remaining rows.

**4.** Sew the rows together, pinning at each seam to keep the blocks and rows aligned. Backstitch at the start and end of each row to reinforce the seams. Press seams open.

See **Quilting + Finishing** to complete your project.

### ASSEMBLY DIAGRAM

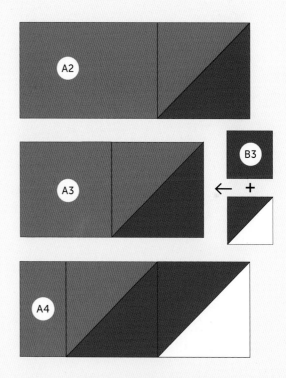

A2

A3    B3
      +
      ←

A4

# CANYON

Now that you've had a go with HSTs, we're heading to the canyon to flex our sewing skills with quarter circle blocks. To ease your way into the glorious world of curves, only four quarter circle blocks are required for this project.

## FINISHED SIZE
40 x 48in

---

## FABRIC REQUIREMENTS

| Fabric | Quantity |
| --- | --- |
| A | ⅜yd or 1 FQ* |
| B | ½yd |
| C | ¼yd or 1 FQ |
| D | ⅜yd |
| E | ⅞yd |
| F | ¼yd or 1 FE |
| Backing | 2¾yds |
| Binding | ⅜yd |

*(1) FQ is sufficient but leaves no room for error

---

## BASIC BLOCKS
Half square triangles (HSTs)
Quarter circles

---

## TEMPLATES
**See Templates** to make the convex and concave quarter circle templates

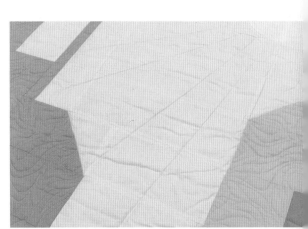

# CUTTING INSTRUCTIONS

- **See Projects** for important notes before you begin.
- Skipped labels (e.g. C2) are intentional.
- Refer to concave and convex cutting instructions **(see Basic Blocks)** for directions on how to cut the fabrics.

## BACKING FABRIC

**Cut 2 pieces** 48in x WOF

## BINDING FABRIC

**Cut 5 pieces** 2½in x WOF

## FABRIC A

**Cut 1 piece** 5in x WOF
**Subcut:**
(1) 5in square **A1**
(1) 12½ x 4½in **A2**
(1) 8½ x 4½in **A3**
**Cut 1 piece** 4½in x WOF
**Subcut:**
(3) 12½ x 4½in **A2**
(1) 4½in square **A4**

**Note:** See cutting diagram if using a FQ for Fabric A.

## FABRIC D

**Cut 1 piece** 5in x WOF
**Subcut:**
(2) 5in squares **D1**
(2) 8½ x 4½in **D3**
(3) 4½in squares **D4**
**Cut 1 piece** 4½in x WOF
**Subcut:**
(3) 12½ x 4½in **D2**

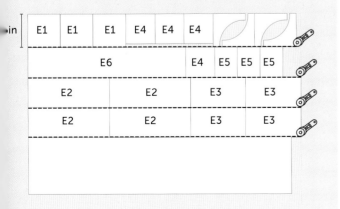

FABRIC A (IF USING A FQ):
CUTTING DIAGRAM

12½in

18in

21in

FABRIC E: CUTTING DIAGRAM

42in WOF

## FABRIC B

**Cut 1 piece** 5in x WOF
**Subcut:**
(4) 5in squares **B1**
**Cut 2 pieces** 4½in x WOF
**Subcut:**
(1) 12½ x 4½in **B2**
(6) 8½ x 4½in **B3**
(2) 4½in squares **B4**
(3) 1½ x 4½in **B5**

## FABRIC C

**Cut 1 piece** 5in x WOF
**Subcut:**
(4) 5in squares **C1**
(1) 8½ x 4½in **C3**
(3) 4½in squares **C4**

## FABRIC E

**Cut 1 piece** 5in x WOF
**Subcut:** see cutting diagram for clarity
(3) 5in squares **E1**
(3) 4½in squares **E4**
(4) Concave pieces
**Cut 3 pieces** 4½in x WOF
**Subcut:**
(1) 24½ x 4½in **E6**
(1) 4½in square **E4**
(3) 3½ x 4½in **E5**
(4) 12½ x 4½in **E2**
(4) 8½ x 4½in **E3**
**Cut 1 piece** 8½in x WOF
**Subcut:**
(1) 40½ x 8½in

## FABRIC F

**Cut 4** convex pieces

## HST CONSTRUCTION

If the total HSTs required is an odd number, there will be an extra HST block. Discard or save for a future project!*

**1.** Pair the following A1–E1 pieces, RST. Refer to HST block instructions (**see Basic Blocks**) to sew and **trim the total HSTs required to 4½in**.

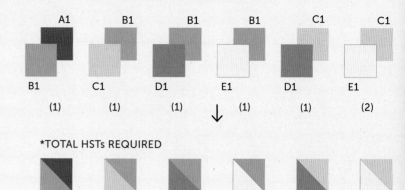

HST CONSTRUCTION

## SPIRE BLOCK CONSTRUCTION

**1.** Sew an E5 piece and a B5 piece along the long edge, RST. Press.

**2.** Repeat the previous step with the remaining E5 and B5 pieces to create a total of (3) BE blocks.

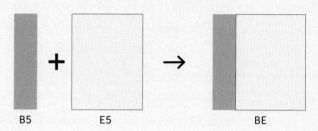

SPIRE BLOCK CONSTRUCTION

## QUARTER CIRCLE BLOCK CONSTRUCTION

**1.** Pair each convex piece with a concave piece. Refer to quarter circle block instructions (**see Basic Blocks**) to sew and **trim each quarter circle block to 4½in**.

**2.** Sew (2) quarter circle blocks to create a half circle unit. Ensure the curved seams are aligned to create a continuous, smooth curve. Press. Repeat with remaining quarter circle blocks to create a total of (2) half circle units.

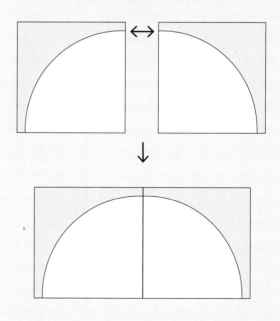

QUARTER CIRCLE BLOCK CONSTRUCTION

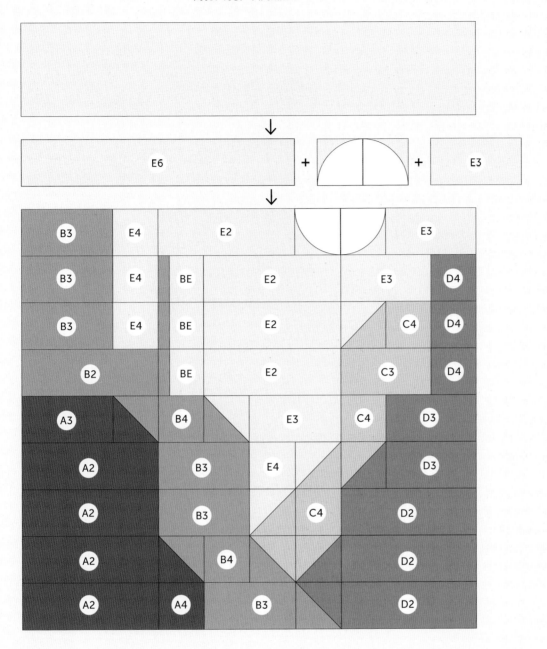

## QUILT TOP ASSEMBLY

**1.** Arrange the blocks as shown in the Assembly Diagram. Ensure the HSTs are properly oriented.

**2.** Sew the blocks into rows. Ensure the curved seams are aligned to create a smooth sun. Press.

**3.** Sew the rows together, pinning at each seam to keep the blocks and rows aligned. Backstitch at the start and end of each row to reinforce the seams. Press seams open.

See **Quilting + Finishing** to complete your project.

### BEHIND THE SCENES

THE COLORS I USED WERE INSPIRED BY THE GOLDEN CANYON NEAR DEATH VALLEY, WHERE MY FAMILY AND I WATCHED THE SUNRISE. UNFORTUNATELY, I MISSED THAT CRUCIAL MOMENT WHEN THE SUN PEEKED FROM THE CANYONS: MY ALLERGIES HAD KICKED IN AND I WAS BUSY GRABBING TISSUES IN THE CAR. SCORE ONE FOR BAD TIMING.

# CANYON MINI

*"It's a butte, Clark, it's a butte."* So this quote's from a popular holiday movie, but I figured the word beaut could double as a nifty way to remember how butte – a rocky, flat-topped hill with steep sides – is pronounced. Speaking of holidays, quilt making tends to kick up several notches around the festive season. I pieced up a couple of samples to represent a quiet, starry night and another using traditional Christmas colors.

## FINISHED SIZE
20 x 24in

---

## FABRIC REQUIREMENTS

| Fabric | Quantity |
|---|---|
| A | ¼yd or 1 FE |
| B | ¼yd or 1 FQ |
| C | ¼yd or 1 FE |
| D | ¼yd or 1 FQ |
| E | ⅜yd or 1 FQ |
| F (with sun) | ¼yd or 1 FE |
| Backing | ¾yd |
| Binding | ¼yd |

---

## BASIC BLOCKS
Half square triangles (HSTs)
Quarter circles

---

## TEMPLATES
**See Templates** to make the convex and concave quarter circle templates

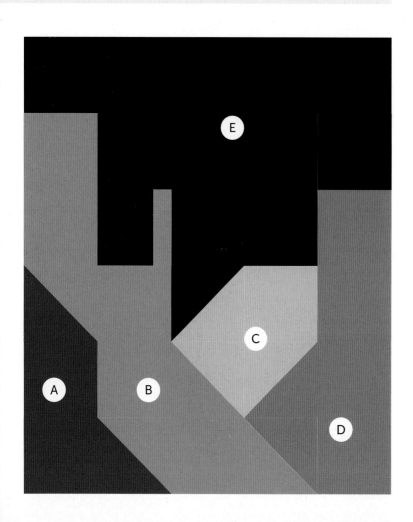

CANYON MINI VERSION WITH OPTIONAL SUN*

## FABRIC A

**Cut 1 piece** 5in x WOF
Subcut:
**(1)** 5in square **A1**
**(2)** 4½in squares **A4**

## FABRIC B

**Cut 1 piece** 5in x WOF
Subcut:
**(3)** 5in squares **B1**
**(5)** 4½in squares **B4**
**(1)** 1½ x 4½in **B5**

## FABRIC C

**Cut 1 piece** 5in x WOF
Subcut:
**(3)** 5in squares **C1**
**(1)** 4½in square **C4**

## FABRIC D

**Cut 1 piece** 5in x WOF
Subcut:
**(2)** 5in squares **D1**
**(4)** 4½in squares **D4**

## FABRIC E

**Cut 1 piece** 5in x WOF
Subcut:
**(1)** 5in square **E1**
**(1)** 8½ x 4½in **E3***
**(2)** 12½ x 4½in **E2**
**(1)** 3½ x 4½in **E5**

**\*If making the sun version:**
Substitute **E3** piece with **(2)** concave pieces.

**Cut 1 piece** 4½in x WOF
Subcut:
**(1)** 8½ x 4½in **E3**
**(1)** 4½in square **E4**

## FABRIC F

**\*If making the sun version:**
**Cut 2** convex pieces

# CUTTING INSTRUCTIONS

- **See Projects** for important notes before you begin.
- Skipped labels (e.g. C2) are intentional.
- Refer to concave and convex cutting instructions (**see Basic Blocks**) for directions on how to cut the fabrics using templates.

## BINDING FABRIC

**Cut 3 pieces** 2½in x WOF

---

HACK ALERT! OMIT THE TOP ROW TO MAKE A SQUARE PILLOW.

---

## HST CONSTRUCTION

If the total HSTs required is an odd number, there will be an extra HST block. Discard or save for a future project!*

**1.** Pair the following A1–E1 pieces, RST. Refer to HST block instructions (**see Basic Blocks**) to sew and **trim the total HSTs required to 4½in**.

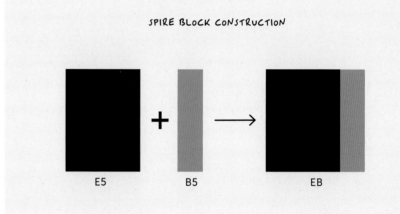

## SPIRE BLOCK CONSTRUCTION

**1.** Sew an E5 piece and a B5 piece along the long edge, RST, to create (1) EB block. Press.

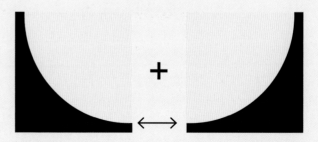

## FOR THE SUN VERSION: QUARTER CIRCLE BLOCK CONSTRUCTION

**1.** Pair each convex piece with a concave piece. Refer to quarter circle block instructions (**see Basic Blocks**) to sew and **trim each quarter circle block to 4½in**.

**2.** Sew the (2) quarter circle blocks to create a half circle unit. Ensure the curved seams are aligned to create a continuous, smooth curve. Press.

ASSEMBLY DIAGRAM

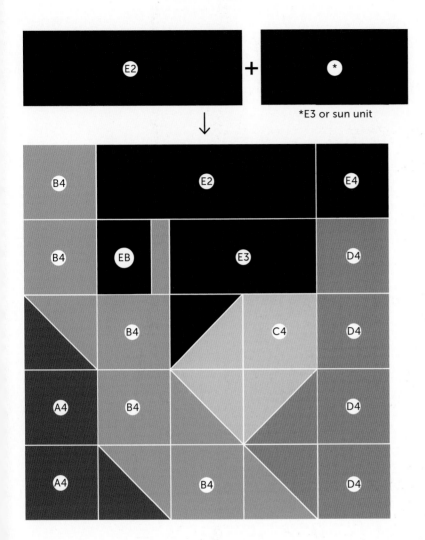

*E3 or sun unit

## QUILT TOP ASSEMBLY

**1.** Arrange the blocks as shown in the Assembly Diagram.

**2.** Sew the blocks into rows. For the sun version, ensure the half circle unit is properly oriented. Press.

**3.** Sew the rows together, pinning at each seam to keep the blocks and rows aligned. Backstitch at the start and end of each row to reinforce the seams. Press seams open.

**See Quilting + Finishing** to complete your project.

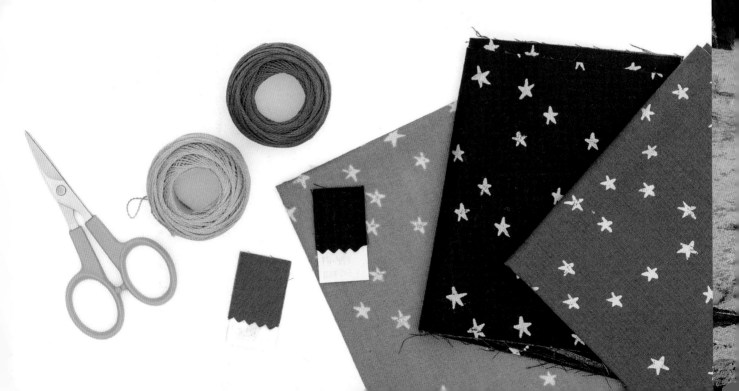

# COASTAL

It's beach time! For this project, we're shifting our attention to strips, both wide and narrow. The bulk of this project uses WOF strips, making it quick-to-piece with minimal fabric waste. Plus, this baby is also versatile. With additional yardage, you can add more strips to make the design longer or wider. Just note that if you do, the sun and the sun glitter will look more distant.

## FINISHED SIZE
41½ x 44½in

---

## FABRIC REQUIREMENTS

| Fabric | Quantity |
|--------|----------|
| A | ⅜yd |
| B | ¼yd |
| C | ¼yd |
| D | ⅜yd |
| E | ½yd |
| F | ⅜yd |
| G | ¼yd |
| Backing | 2⅞yds |
| Binding | ⅜yd |

---

## BASIC BLOCKS
Strips
Quarter circles

---

## TEMPLATES
**See Templates** to make the convex and concave quarter circle templates

**FABRIC A**

**Cut 1 piece** 9in x WOF

**FABRIC B**

**Cut 1 piece** 5½in x WOF

**FABRIC C**

**Cut 1 piece** 6½in x WOF

**FABRIC D**

**Cut 1 piece** 7½in x WOF
**Subcut:**
**(2)** 17¼ x 7½in **D1**
**(2)** concave pieces
**Cut 1 piece** 3½in x WOF
**Subcut:**
**(1)** 8½ x 3½in **D2**

**FABRIC E**

**Cut 1 piece** 8½in x WOF
**Subcut:**
**(2)** 7¾ x 8½in **E5**
**Cut 4 pieces** 1½in x WOF
**Subcut:**
**(4)** 27½ x 1½in **E1**
**(2)** 9¼ x 1½in **E2**
**(2)** 7 x 1½in **E3**
**(2)** 5 x 1½in **E4**

**FABRIC F**

**Cut 1 piece** 10½in x WOF

**FABRIC G**

**Cut 1 piece** 4½in x WOF
**Subcut:**
**(2)** convex pieces
**(1)** 27½ x 1½in **G1**
**(1)** 18½ x 1½in **G4**
**(1)** 14½ x 1½in **G3**
**(1)** 10 x 1½in **G2**

# CUTTING INSTRUCTIONS

- **See Projects** for important notes before you begin.
- Remember to trim the selvages of Fabrics A, B, C, and F before assembly to ensure the 42in WOF.
- Pay extra close attention to fractions before cutting.
- Refer to concave and convex cutting instructions (**see Basic Blocks**) for directions on how to cut the fabrics using templates.

## BACKING FABRIC

**Cut 2 pieces** 51¾in x WOF

## BINDING FABRIC

**Cut 5 pieces** 2½in x WOF

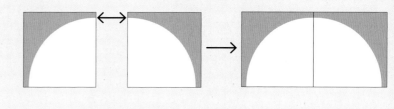

## SUN ROW CONSTRUCTION

**1.** Refer to quarter circle block instructions (**see Basic Blocks**) to sew and **trim each quarter circle block to 4½in**.

**2.** Sew (2) quarter circle blocks to create a half circle unit. Ensure the curved seams are aligned to create a continuous, smooth curve. Press seams open.

**3.** Refer to the Assembly Diagram. Sew the D2 piece above the half circle unit to complete the sun block unit. Press. Sew a D1 piece to each side of the sun block unit to complete the sun row. Press seams open.

## OCEAN ROW CONSTRUCTION

Refer to strip instructions (**see Basic Blocks**) for important sewing tips.

**1.** Sew one E2, E3, and E4 strip to each side of the corresponding G2, G3, and G4 strip. Press seams open.

**2.** Arrange the E and G strips as shown. Sew the strips together to create a 27½ x 8½in strip, pinning at each seam to keep the strips aligned and alternating the directions you feed your strips when sewing to prevent them from bowing. Press seams open as you go.

---

**PERFECTING STRIPS:** SEWING STRIPS TOGETHER ACCURATELY CAN TAKE SOME PRACTICE. IF YOUR STRIP UNIT IS NOT QUITE 8½IN TALL, TRIM YOUR E5 PIECES TO MATCH AND ACCOMMODATE THE HEIGHT OF YOUR SHORTER-THAN-EXPECTED STRIP UNIT.

---

**3.** Sew an E5 piece to each side of the strip to complete the ocean row. Press.

OCEAN ROW CONSTRUCTION

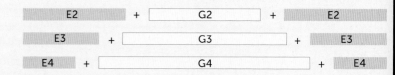

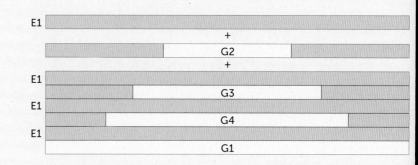

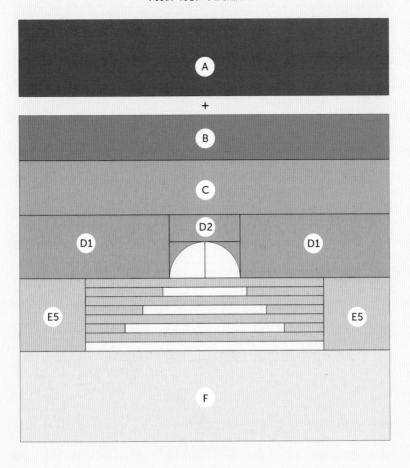

## BEHIND THE SCENES

AS SIMPLE AS THE DESIGN LOOKS, THIS WAS ACTUALLY THE MOST CHALLENGING PROJECT TO CONCEPTUALIZE. AFTER THE INITIAL SKETCH, TOO MANY HOURS WERE SPENT RESEARCHING AND OVERTHINKING THE GLITTER PATH LAYOUT: DOES IT GET NARROW OR SPREAD OUTWARD? TURNS OUT, BOTH ARE CORRECT! THAT'S WHY YOU MIGHT NOTICE THE DIFFERENT GLITTER PATH BETWEEN THIS PROJECT AND ITS MINI VERSION.

## QUILT TOP ASSEMBLY

**1.** Arrange the blocks as shown in the Assembly Diagram.

**2.** Sew the rows together, pinning at each seam to keep the blocks and rows aligned. Backstitch at the start and end of each row to reinforce the seams. Press seams open.

See **Quilting + Finishing** to complete your project.

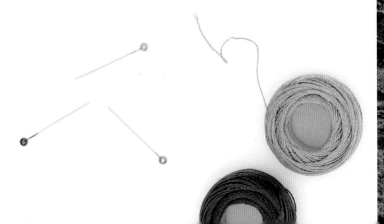

# COASTAL MINI

The generous negative space surrounding the design allows you to use it as a springboard for other projects. For instance, simply cut the sides equally to your desired size to make placemats. If you're a seasoned quilter, the pieced top can be turned into a quilted tote bag, laptop case, or the back of a quilt coat. Go forth and flex your creative muscle!

## FINISHED SIZE
20 x 20in

---

## FABRIC REQUIREMENTS

| Fabric | Quantity |
|---|---|
| A | ¼yd or 1 FQ |
| B | ¼yd or 1 FQ |
| C | ¼yd or 1 FE |

**For mini quilt:**

| | |
|---|---|
| Backing | ¾yd |
| Binding | ¼yd |

**For pillow:**

| | |
|---|---|
| Backing | ⅜yd |
| Binding | n/a |

---

## BASIC BLOCKS
Strips
Quarter circles

---

## TEMPLATES
**See Templates** to make the convex and concave quarter circle templates

# CUTTING INSTRUCTIONS

- **See Projects** for important notes before you begin.
- Skipped labels (e.g. C1 and C2) are intentional.

## MINI QUILT BINDING FABRIC

**Cut 3 pieces** 2½in x WOF

## PILLOW BACKING FABRIC

**Cut 1 piece** 13½in x WOF
**Subcut:**
**(2)** 20½ x 14¼in

### FABRIC A

**Cut 1 piece** 6½in x WOF
**Subcut:**
**(2)** 10½ x 6½in **A1**
**(1)** 8½ x 6½in **A2**
**(2)** concave pieces

### FABRIC C

**Cut 1 piece** 4½in x WOF
**Subcut:**
**(2)** convex pieces
**(1)** 8½ x 1½in **C3**
**(1)** 4½ x 1½in **C4**
**(1)** 6½ x 1½in **C5**

### FABRIC B

**Cut 1 piece** 6½in x WOF
**Subcut:** see cutting diagram for clarity
**(2)** 10½ x 6½in **B1**
**(1)** 8½ x 4½in **B2**
**(3)** 8½ x 1½in **B3**
**(2)** 2½ x 1½in **B4**
**(2)** 1½in **B5**

FABRIC B: CUTTING DIAGRAM

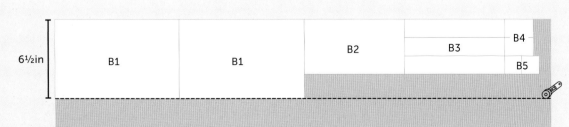

6½in

B1    B1    B2    B3    B4    B5

42in WOF

## SKY UNIT CONSTRUCTION

**1.** Refer to quarter circle block instructions (**see Basic Blocks**) to sew and **trim each quarter circle block to 4½in**.

**2.** Sew (2) quarter circle blocks to create the half circle unit. Ensure the curved seams are aligned to create a continuous, smooth curve. Press seams open.

**3.** Sew the A2 piece above the half circle unit. Press. Sew an A1 piece to each side of the half circle unit to complete the sky unit. Press seams open.

## OCEAN UNIT CONSTRUCTION

Refer to strip instructions (**see Basic Blocks**) for important sewing tips.

**1.** Sew a B4 and B5 piece to each side of the corresponding C4 and C5 piece. Press seams open.

**2.** Arrange the B and C strips as shown. Sew the strips together to create a **10½in tall strip**, pinning at each seam to keep the strips aligned and alternating the directions you feed your strips through your machine when sewing to prevent them from bowing. Press seams open as you go.

**3.** Refer to the Assembly Diagram. Sew a B1 piece to each side of the strip to complete the ocean unit. Press seams open.

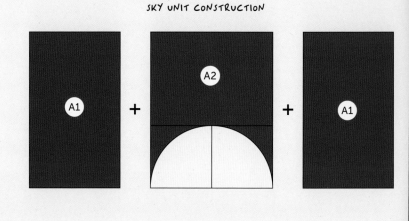

SKY UNIT CONSTRUCTION

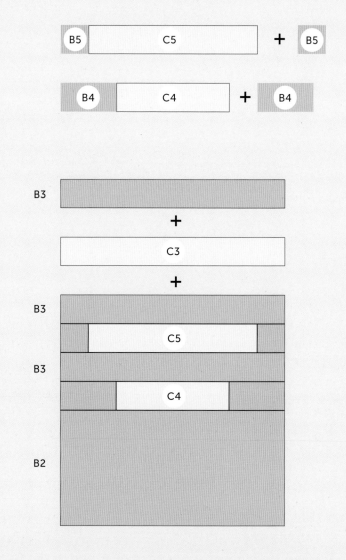

OCEAN UNIT CONSTRUCTION

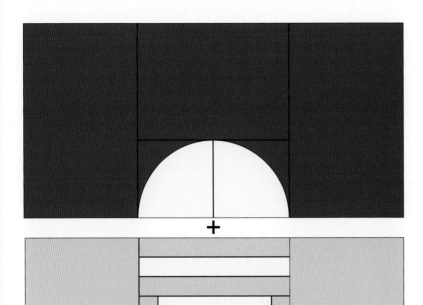

## QUILT TOP ASSEMBLY

**1.** Sew the sky and ocean unit together to complete the quilt top. Press seams open.

See **Quilting + Finishing** to complete your project.

HACK ALERT! TRIM AWAY 3 INCHES FROM THE TOP AND BOTTOM OF YOUR QUILT TOP TO CREATE A CHIC PLACEMAT. REFER TO FINISHING A QUILT TO VIEW A SAMPLE.

# RIVER

We're going up the river *with* a paddle for this next stop in our adventure. Equilateral triangles are used exclusively to create this project and are great practice for working with bias edges. Just be mindful about your triangle placement as it can create unintentional mountains alongside the river.

## FINISHED SIZE
46½ x 57½in

---

## FABRIC REQUIREMENTS

| Fabric | Quantity |
| --- | --- |
| A | 1½yds* |
| B | ⅝yd |
| C | ½yd |
| D | ½yd |
| E | ¾yd |
| Backing | 3⅛yds |
| Binding | ½yd |

*For scrappy roadside option:
A1: ⅝yd
A2: ⅝yd
A3: ½yd

---

## TEMPLATES
See Templates to make the 6½in triangle template.

# CUTTING INSTRUCTIONS

- **See Projects** for important notes before you begin.
- Seam allowance is ¼in, but you might prefer a scant ¼in seam allowance to sew the triangles together.

### BACKING FABRIC
**Cut 2 pieces** 56¼in x WOF

### BINDING FABRIC
**Cut 6 pieces** 2½in x WOF

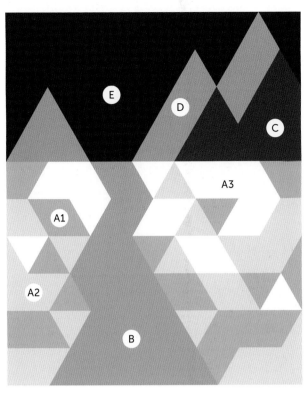

SCRAPPY ROADSIDE OPTION

**FABRIC A***

Cut 8 pieces 6½in x WOF

**FABRIC D**

Cut 2 pieces 6½in x WOF

**FABRIC B**

Cut 3 pieces 6½in x WOF

**FABRIC E**

Cut 4 pieces 6½in x WOF

**FABRIC C**

Cut 2 pieces 6½in x WOF

## *SCRAPPY ROADSIDE OPTION

**Fabric A1: Cut 3 pieces** 6½in x WOF
**Fabric A2: Cut 3 pieces** 6½in x WOF
**Fabric A3: Cut 2 pieces** 6½in x WOF

**SCRAPPY LOOK:** IF YOU'RE GOING THE SCRAPPY ROUTE, OPT FOR SOLIDS OR LOW VOLUME PRINTS THAT WILL BE DISTINCT FROM YOUR MOUNTAIN AND RIVER COLORS. THIS ENSURES THE LANDSCAPE FEATURES ARE NOT VISUALLY IMPACTED.

## TRIANGLES

Each WOF strip yields **9 triangles**.

Handle triangles with extra care as bias edges tend to stretch easily.

The colors used in this section are for visual clarity and therefore, do not reflect the fabric colors of the project.

**1.** Place a Fabric A WOF strip on the cutting mat, folded in half with fabric ends together so you can cut two triangles at a time! Place your template as close to the fabric ends as possible. Cut the fabric along the sides of the template. Rotate the template 180-degrees and line it up against the edge of your last cut. Cut the fabric along the template. Continue until you've cut 8 triangles from the folded WOF strip. Unfold and gently press the remaining WOF strip to cut the ninth triangle.

**2.** Repeat step 1 as needed to yield the following number of triangles:

| | |
|---|---|
| **A\*** = 67 | *For the scrappy |
| **B** = 23 | roadside option: |
| **C** = 11 | **A1** = 23 |
| **D** = 13 | **A2** = 27 |
| **E** = 36 | **A3** = 17 |

## ROW CONSTRUCTION

You may choose to trim the dog ears after step 4, but it's an extra step that will not considerably reduce bulk. I recommend saving time by keeping the dog ears intact; they can also act as an alignment guide when sewing rows together.

**1.** Arrange the triangles as shown in the Assembly Diagram. Sew the first two triangles of the first row, RST, as shown. Gently finger press the seam open.

---

**NOTE:** PRESSING THE SEAM WITH YOUR FINGER ELIMINATES THE REPETITIVE TRIPS TO THE IRONING BOARD AS YOU SEW THE TRIANGLES INTO ROWS.

---

**2.** Lay your third triangle on the top of your second triangle, RST, aligning the right edges. When aligning, one corner of the triangle will have a ¼in overhang. Sew together along the edge. Gently finger press the seam open.

**3.** Continue adding triangles until the row is complete.

**4.** Repeat steps 1–3 with remaining rows. Once all the rows are constructed, gently press the seams with an iron.

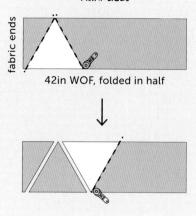

TRIANGLES

fabric ends

42in WOF, folded in half

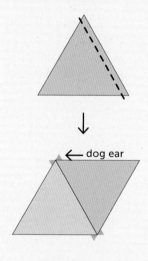

ROW CONSTRUCTION (STEP 1)

← dog ear

ROW CONSTRUCTION (STEP 2)

¼in overhang

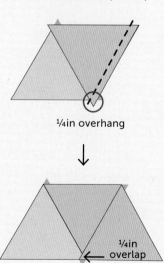

¼in overlap

ASSEMBLY DIAGRAM

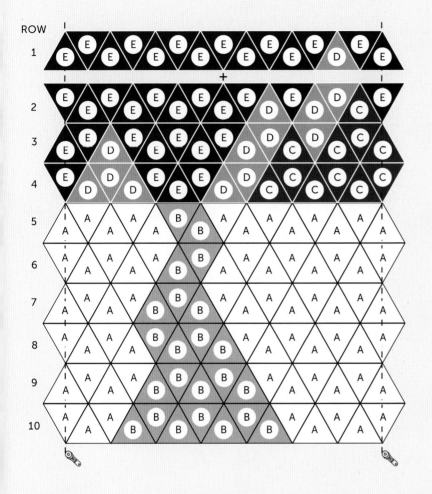

## QUILT TOP ASSEMBLY

**1.** Sew the rows together, matching the seams and pinning at the triangle points. Line up the dog ears as an extra guide to keep your triangles aligned. Backstitch at the start and end of each row to reinforce the seams. Press seams open.

**2.** Trim the sides, leaving a ¼in seam allowance to make room for the binding.

See **Quilting + Finishing** to complete your project.

### BEHIND THE SCENES

THE SCRAPPY OPTION WAS ADDED AS AN ANSWER TO MY DESIRE TO JAZZ UP THE CONSTRUCTION PROCESS AND MAKE USE OF THE LEFTOVER FABRICS FROM PREVIOUS PROJECTS. AFTER MAKING BOTH SAMPLES, I FOUND MYSELF PREFERRING THE SCRAPPY VERSION. I LOVE HOW IT ADDS A RUGGED, IMPERFECT LOOK TO THE LANDSCAPE.

SCRAPPY ROADSIDE OPTION

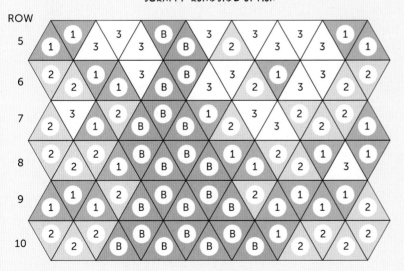

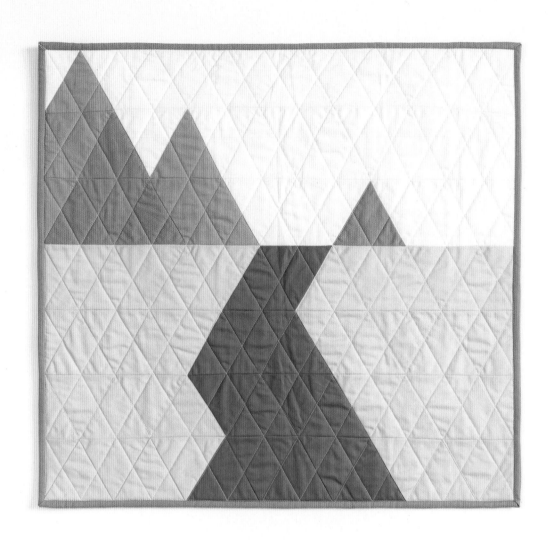

# RIVER MINI

Unlike its bigger version, the River Mini doesn't include a scrappy diagram. Let your artistic side run wild and try making the river scrappy instead. This is also the only project in the book where the finished size is wider than it is tall. Feel free to cut the sides equally to make it a square. Your project, your rules.

## FINISHED SIZE
24½ x 22¾in approx

---

## FABRIC REQUIREMENTS

| Fabric | Quantity |
| --- | --- |
| A | ⅜yd |
| B | ¼yd or 1 FE |
| C | ¼yd or 1 FE |
| D | ¼yd or 1 FE |
| E | ¼yd or 1 FQ |
| Backing | ⅞yd |
| Binding | ¼yd |

---

## TEMPLATES
**See Templates** to make the 4in triangle template.

# CUTTING INSTRUCTIONS

- **See Projects** for important notes before you begin.
- Seam allowance is ¼in, but you might prefer a scant ¼in seam allowance to sew the triangles together.

## BINDING FABRIC

**Cut 3 pieces** 2½in x WOF

**FABRIC A**

**Cut 3 pieces** 4in x WOF

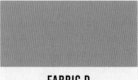

**FABRIC D**

**Cut 1 piece** 4in x WOF

**FABRIC B**

**Cut 1 piece** 4in x WOF

**FABRIC E**

**Cut 2 pieces** 4in x WOF

**FABRIC C**

**Cut 1 piece** 4in x WOF

## TRIANGLES

Each WOF strip yields **17 triangles**.

Handle triangles with extra care as bias edges tend to stretch easily.

For precut fabrics, a 21in long strip yields 8 triangles. **Do not fold precut fabrics in half (as instructed in step 1), as it will not yield enough triangles.**

The colors used in this section are for visual clarity and therefore, do not reflect the fabric colors of the project.

**1.** Place a Fabric A WOF strip on the cutting mat, folded in half with fabric ends together so you can cut two triangles at a time! Place your template as close to the fabric ends as possible. Cut the fabric along the sides of the template. Rotate the template 180-degrees and line it up against the edge of your last cut. Cut the fabric along the template. If making more than 16 triangles in one WOF strip, unfold and gently press the remaining WOF strip to cut the seventeenth triangle.

**2.** Repeat step 1 as needed to yield the following number of triangles:

**A** = 42
**B** = 14
**C** = 5
**D** = 7
**E** = 30

## ROW CONSTRUCTION

You may choose to trim the dog ears after step 4, but it's an extra step that will not considerably reduce bulk. I recommend saving time by keeping the dog ears intact; they can also act as an alignment guide when sewing rows together.

**1.** Arrange the triangles as shown in the Assembly Diagram. Sew the first two triangles of the first row, RST, as shown. Gently finger press the seam open.

---

**NOTE:** PRESSING THE SEAM WITH YOUR FINGER ELIMINATES THE REPETITIVE TRIPS TO THE IRONING BOARD AS YOU SEW THE TRIANGLES INTO ROWS.

---

**2.** Lay your third triangle on the top of your second triangle, RST, aligning the right edges. When aligning, one corner of the triangle will have a ¼in overlap. Sew together along the edge. Gently finger press the seam open.

**3.** Continue adding triangles until the row is complete.

**4.** Repeat steps 1–3 with remaining rows. Once all the rows are constructed, gently press the seams with an iron.

TRIANGLES

fabric ends

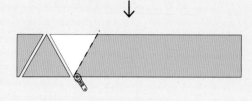

42in WOF, folded in half (do not fold if using precut fabric)

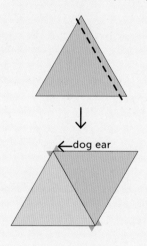

ROW CONSTRUCTION (STEP 1)

←dog ear

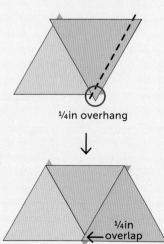

ROW CONSTRUCTION (STEP 2)

¼in overhang

¼in
←overlap

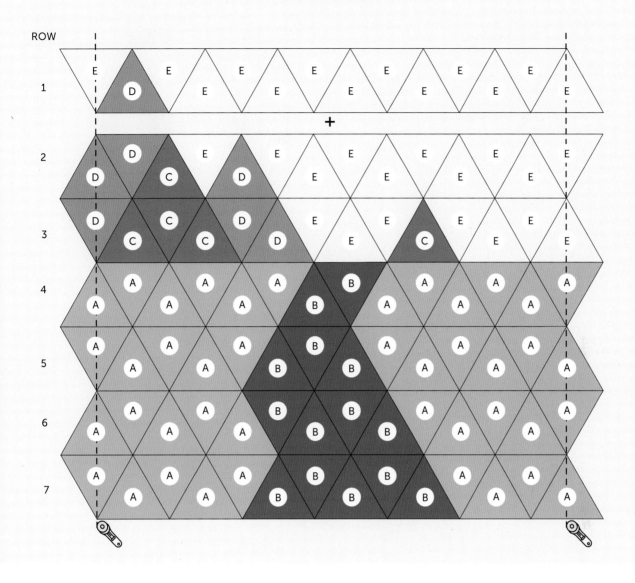

## QUILT TOP ASSEMBLY

**1.** Sew the rows together, matching the seams and pinning at the triangle points. Line up the dog ears as an extra guide to keep your triangles aligned. Backstitch at the start and end of each row to reinforce the seams. Press seams open.

**2.** Trim the sides, leaving a ¼in seam allowance to make room for the binding.

See **Quilting + Finishing** to complete your project.

# MEADOW

We're driving through the Meadow with this generously sized throw. We'll dive into a mix of HSTs and strips, as well as introduce you to strip piecing and snowball corners. These two techniques provide a quick shortcut to assemble your quilt top in a jiffy. To achieve proper perspective, use a darker color for the closest hill, a medium color for the middle, and a lighter color for the farthest hill. For more guidance on color selection, **see Choosing Colors**.

## FINISHED SIZE
72 x 72in

---

## FABRIC REQUIREMENTS

| Fabric | Quantity |
| --- | --- |
| A | 2¼yds |
| B | ⅜yd |
| C | ¼yd or 1 FE |
| D | ⅛yd, or 1 FE, or 5in square scrap |
| E | ⅝yd |
| F | ⅝yd |
| G | ¾yd |
| H | ⅜yd or 1 FE* |
| J | ⅜yd or 1 FE* |
| K | ⅝yd |
| Backing | 4½yds |
| Binding | ⅝yd |

Letter "I" is skipped to avoid confusion.

*FE is sufficient but leaves no room for error.

---

## BASIC BLOCKS
Half square triangles (HSTs)
Strips

# CUTTING INSTRUCTIONS

- **See Projects** for important notes before you begin.
- Skipped labels (e.g. G3) are intentional.

## BACKING FABRIC

**Cut 2 pieces** 81in x WOF

## BINDING FABRIC

**Cut 8 pieces** 2½in x WOF

### FABRIC A

**Cut 5 pieces** 8½in x WOF
**Subcut:**
**(1)** 36½ x 8½in **A1**
**(1)** 32½ x 8½in **A2**
**(2)** 24½ x 8½in **A3**
**(1)** 20½ x 8½in **A4**
**(2)** 8½in squares **A5**
**(1)** 12½ x 4½in **A13**
**(2)** 5½ x 4½in **A14**
**(4)** 2½in squares **A15**

**Cut 2 pieces** 6½in x WOF
**Cut 3 pieces** 4½in x WOF
**Cut 3 pieces** 2½in x WOF

### FABRIC B

**Cut 5 pieces** 2½in x WOF

### FABRIC C

**Cut 1 piece** 12½ x 8½in

### FABRIC D

**Cut 1 piece** 2½ x 4½in

### FABRIC E

**Cut 1 piece** 9in x WOF
**Subcut:**
**(1)** 9in square **E1**
**(1)** 32½ x 8½in **E2**

**Cut 1 piece** 8½in x WOF
**Subcut:**
**(1)** 16½ x 8½in **E3**
**(1)** 4½ x 8½in **E4**

### FABRIC F

**Cut 1 piece** 9in x WOF
**Subcut:**
**(1)** 9in square **F1**
**(1)** 32½ x 8½in **F2**

**Cut 1 piece** 8½in x WOF
**Subcut:**
**(1)** 16½ x 8½in **F3**

### FABRIC G

**Cut 1 piece** 9in x WOF
**Subcut:**
**(2)** 9in squares **G1**

**Cut 2 pieces** 8½in x WOF
**Subcut:**
**(2)** 32½ x 8½in **G2**
**(1)** 8½in square **G5**

### FABRIC H

**Cut 1 piece** 9in x WOF
**Subcut:**
**(1)** 9in square **H1**
**(1)** 4½ x 8½in **H4**

### FABRIC J

**Cut 1 piece** 9in x WOF
**Subcut:**
**(1)** 9in square **J1**
**(1)** 8½in square **J5**

### FABRIC K

**Cut 1 piece** 9in x WOF
**Subcut:**
**(2)** 9in squares **K1**
**(1)** 16½ x 8½in **K3**

**Cut 1 piece** 8½in x WOF
**Subcut:**
**(1)** 32½ x 8½in **K2**

## TREE UNIT CONSTRUCTION

**1.** Mark a diagonal line on the wrong side of each A15 square. Position each A15 square on the C piece, RST, as shown. Sew just outside the line (towards the C piece corners) to account for fabric loss after the seams are pressed. Trim all corners ¼in away from the seams and discard the triangle pieces, as demonstrated in one corner of the second diagram. Press.

**2.** Sew an A14 piece on each 4½in side of the D piece to create the trunk unit. Press. Sew the trunk unit to the tree canopy unit. Sew the A13 piece above to complete the tree unit. Press.

## SKY CONSTRUCTION

Refer to strip instructions (**see Basic Blocks**) for important sewing tips and an overview of the strip piecing method.

**1.** Sew the following WOF strips together as shown: A, 2½in; B, 2½in; A, 4½in. Repeat two more times to create a total of three strip sets. The height should measure **8½in**. Press seams open.

**2.** Subcut the three strip sets to the following widths and label accordingly:

**(1)** 40½in **A6**

**(1)** 36½in **A7**

**(1)** 32½in **A8**

**(1)** 8½in **A9**

**3.** Sew the following WOF strips together as shown: B, 2½in; A, 6½in. Repeat once to create a total of two strip sets. The height should measure **8½in**. Press seams open.

**4.** Subcut the two strip sets to the following widths and label accordingly:

**(2)** 24½in **A10**

**(1)** 12½in **A11**

**(1)** 8½in **A12**

## HST CONSTRUCTION

There will be an extra G/K HST block. Discard or save for a future project!

**1.** Pair the following E1-K1 pieces, RST. Refer to HST block instructions (**see Basic Blocks**) to sew and **trim the total HSTs required to 8½in**.

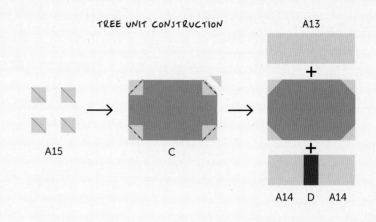

TREE UNIT CONSTRUCTION

A13

A15     C     A14  D  A14

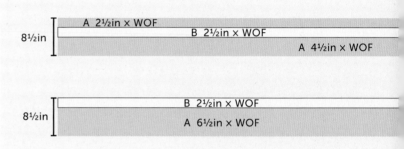

SKY CONSTRUCTION

8½in    A  2½in × WOF
        B  2½in × WOF
                    A  4½in × WOF

8½in    B  2½in × WOF
        A  6½in × WOF

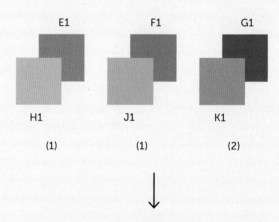

HST CONSTRUCTION

E1          F1          G1

H1          J1          K1

(1)         (1)         (2)

↓

TOTAL HSTs REQUIRED

(2)         (2)         (3)

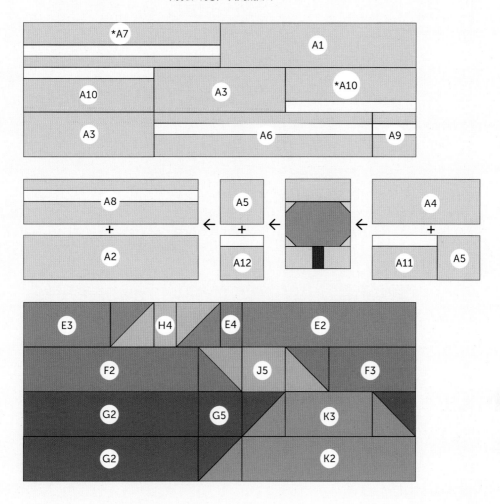

## QUILT TOP ASSEMBLY

**1.** Arrange the blocks as shown in the Assembly Diagram. Ensure HSTs are in their proper orientation.

**2.** First, sew the tree rows as indicated with a + symbol in the Assembly Diagram. Press.

**3.** Sew the remaining blocks into rows. Press. **Note\*:** the A7 piece and (1) A10 piece will be sewn upside down.

**4.** Sew the rows together, pinning at each seam to keep the blocks and rows aligned. Backstitch at the start and end of each row to reinforce the seams. Press seams open.

See **Quilting + Finishing** to complete your project.

### BEHIND THE SCENES

FULL DISCLOSURE: I ALMOST SCRAPPED THIS DESIGN BECAUSE IT WAS LOOKING A BIT TOO 8-BIT FOR MY LIKING! IT STARTED WITH A LOT OF TREES, BUT THAT THEME IS COVERED WITH THE WOODLAND PROJECT. HOWEVER, AS I WAS SEWING UP THIS SAMPLE, I REALIZED HOW MUCH FUN I HAD PIECING IT TOGETHER! IT WAS INCREDIBLY SATISFYING ASSEMBLING THE QUILT TOP AND I'VE COME TO REALLY APPRECIATE IT, ESPECIALLY KNOWING IT'S ONE OF MY GIRLS' FAVORITES OF THE BUNCH. THEY LOVE THE VIDEO GAME FEEL TO IT. SO THERE YOU GO: IF YOU'RE THINKING OF MAKING ONE FOR A CHILD, THIS IS KID-APPROVED.

# MEADOW MINI

Feel the breeze because this one is thoughtfully designed for a fast make. Even though the rolling countryside is removed, the lone tree from afar and the fresh strips of clouds help convey a minimal, scenic meadow. In addition, you can choose to complete your project as a large pillow or a wall hanging. We're all about choosing our own path over here.

## FINISHED SIZE

24 x 24in pillow or
24 x 30in mini

## FABRIC REQUIREMENTS

| Fabric | Quantity |
| --- | --- |
| A | ½yd |
| B | ¼yd |
| C | ¼yd or 1 FE |
| D | ⅛yd, or 1 FE, or 4in square scrap |
| E (for mini quilt only) | ¼yd |

| For mini quilt: | |
| --- | --- |
| Backing | ⅞yd |
| Binding | ¼yd |

| For pillow: | |
| --- | --- |
| Backing | ¾yd |

## BASIC BLOCK
Strips

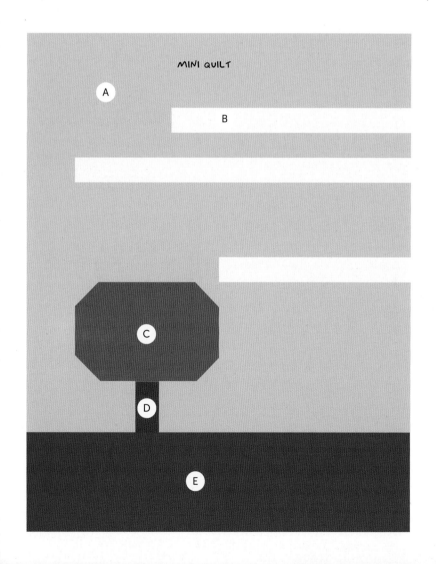

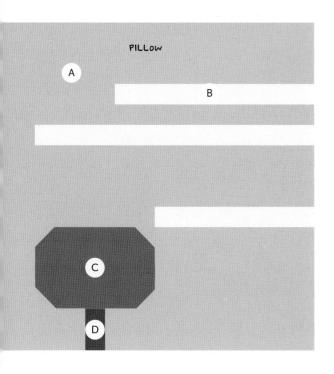

PILLOW

**FABRIC A**

Cut 1 piece 6½in x WOF
Subcut:
(1) 12½ x 6½in **A1**
(1) 9½ x 6½in **A2**
(1) 15½ x 5in **A3**
(4) 2in squares **A9**

Cut 2 pieces 3½in x WOF
Subcut (1) strip to:
(1) 18½ x 3½in **A6**
(1) 9½ x 3½in **A7**
(2) 4¼ x 3½in **A8**

Cut 1 piece 2in x WOF

**FABRIC C**

Cut 1 piece 9½ x 6½in

**FABRIC D**

Cut 1 piece 2 x 3½in

**FABRIC E**

If making the mini quilt
version only:
Cut 1 piece 24½ x 6½in

**FABRIC B**

Cut 1 piece 2in x WOF
Cut 1 piece  15½ x 2in **B3**

# CUTTING INSTRUCTIONS

- **See Projects** for important notes before
  you begin.
- Skipped labels (e.g. B1) are intentional.
- Pay extra close attention to fractions
  before cutting.

## BACKING FABRIC FOR PILLOW

Cut 2 pieces 24½ x 16¼in

## BINDING FABRIC FOR MINI QUILT

Cut 3 pieces 2½in x WOF

## TREE UNIT CONSTRUCTION

**1.** Mark a diagonal line on the wrong side of each A9 square. Position each A9 square on the C piece, RST, as shown. Sew just outside the line (towards the C piece corners) to account for fabric loss after the seams are pressed. Trim all corners ¼in away from the seams and discard the triangle pieces, as demonstrated in one corner of the second diagram. Press.

**2.** Sew an A8 piece on each 3½in side of the D piece to create the trunk unit. Press. Sew the trunk unit to the tree canopy unit. Sew the A7 piece above to complete the tree unit. Press.

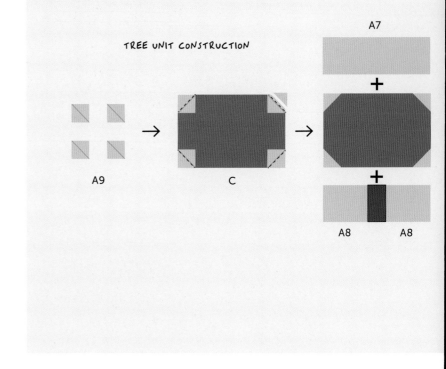

TREE UNIT CONSTRUCTION

A9     C     A7

A8     A8

## SKY CONSTRUCTION

Refer to strip instructions (**see Basic Blocks**) for important sewing tips and an overview of the strip piecing method.

**1.** Sew the following three WOF strips together as shown: A, 2in; B, 2in; A, 3½in. The height should measure **6½in**. Press seams open.

**2.** Subcut the strip set to the following widths and label accordingly:

**(1)** 21½in **A4**

**(1)** 12½in **A5**

**3.** Sew the A3 piece and the B3 piece along the long edge, RST, to complete the A3 unit. Press seams open.

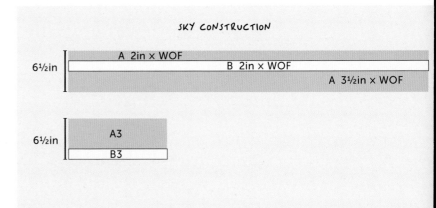

SKY CONSTRUCTION

6½in    A 2in × WOF

B 2in × WOF

A 3½in × WOF

6½in    A3

B3

ASSEMBLY DIAGRAM

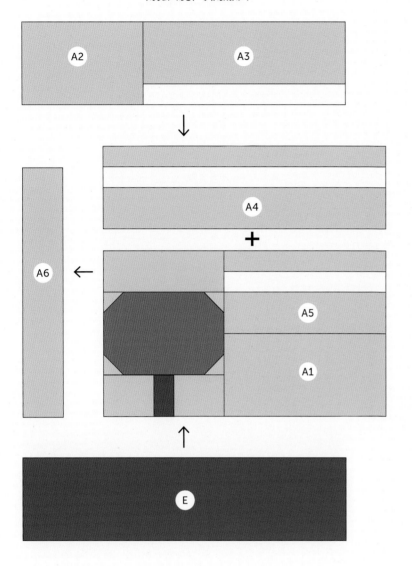

## QUILT TOP ASSEMBLY

**1.** Arrange the blocks as shown in the Assembly Diagram.

**2.** Sew the A2 piece and A3 piece together. Press seams open.

**3.** Sew the A5 piece and A1 piece together. Press seams open and then sew to the right of the tree unit. Press seams open.

**4.** Sew the A4 piece to the top of the tree unit. Press seams open.

**5.** Sew the A6 piece to the left of the assembled unit from step 4. Press seams open. Then, sew the top row to complete the pillow quilt top. Press seams open.

**6.** If making the mini quilt version: Sew the E piece to the bottom of the quilt top. Press seams open.

See **Quilting + Finishing** to complete your project.

# MOUNTAIN

Now it's time to switch gears as we head to the Mountain with HRTs! We're kicking things up a notch with this versatile basic block. HRTs get a bit of a bad rap for being more rebellious and puzzling than their HST cousin. For this project, we're going to remove its trench coat and sunglasses to demystify this endlessly cool block once and for all.

## FINISHED SIZE
55 x 60in

———

## FABRIC REQUIREMENTS

| Fabric | Quantity |
|---|---|
| A | ⅜yd |
| B | ⅞yd |
| C | ¾yd |
| D | ½yd |
| E | ⅝yd |
| F | 1yd |
| Backing | 3½yds |
| Binding | ⅝yd |

———

## BASIC BLOCKS
Half rectangle triangles (HRTs)
Half square triangles (HSTs)

# CUTTING INSTRUCTIONS

- **See Projects** for important notes before you begin.

## BACKING FABRIC
**Cut 2 pieces** 63in x WOF

## BINDING FABRIC
**Cut 7 pieces** 2½in x WOF

### FABRIC C

**Cut 2 pieces** 6in x WOF
Subcut:
**(4)** 12 x 6in **C1**
**(5)** 6in squares **C2**
**Cut 2 pieces** 5½in x WOF
Subcut:
**(4)** 10½ x 5½in **C4**
**(4)** 5½in squares **C3**

### FABRIC E

**Cut 2 pieces** 6in x WOF
Subcut:
**(3)** 12 x 6in **E1**
**(3)** 6in squares **E2**
**(2)** 5½in squares **E3**
**Cut 1 piece** 5½in x WOF
Subcut:
**(3)** 10½ x 5½in **E4**

### FABRIC A

**Cut 1 piece** 6in x WOF
Subcut:
**(2)** 12 x 6in **A1**
**(1)** 6in square **A2**
**(2)** 5½in squares **A3**
**Cut 1 piece** 5½in x WOF
Subcut:
**(1)** 20½ x 5½in **A5**
**(1)** 10½ x 5½in **A4**
**(1)** 5½in square **A3**

### FABRIC B

**Cut 2 pieces** 6in x WOF
Subcut:
**(4)** 12 x 6in **B1**
**(4)** 6in squares **B2**
**Cut 3 pieces** 5½in x WOF
Subcut:
**(2)** 20½ x 5½in **B5**
**(4)** 10½ x 5½in **B4**
**(4)** 5½in squares **B3**

### FABRIC D

**Cut 1 piece** 6in x WOF
Subcut:
**(2)** 12 x 6in **D1**
**(3)** 6in squares **D2**
**Cut 2 pieces** 5½in x WOF
Subcut:
**(3)** 10½ x 5½in **D4**
**(2)** 5½in squares **D3**

### FABRIC F

**Cut 1 piece** 6in x WOF
Subcut:
**(2)** 6in squares **F2**
**(4)** 5½in squares **F3**
**Cut 1 piece** 5½in x WOF
Subcut:
**(1)** 20½ x 5½in **F5**
**(1)** 10½ x 5½in **F4**
**Cut 2 pieces** 10½in x WOF
Subcut one strip to:
**(1)** 14 x 10½in **F6**
**(2)** 12 x 6in **F1**

## HST CONSTRUCTION

If the total HSTs required is an odd number, there will be an extra HST block. Discard or save for a future project!*

**1.** Pair the following A2-F2 pieces, RST. Refer to HST block instructions to sew and **trim the total HSTs required to 5½in.**

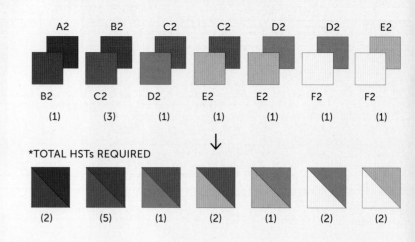

HST CONSTRUCTION DIAGRAM

| A2 | B2 | C2 | C2 | D2 | D2 | E2 |
| B2 | C2 | D2 | E2 | E2 | F2 | F2 |
| (1) | (3) | (1) | (1) | (1) | (1) | (1) |

↓

*TOTAL HSTs REQUIRED

| (2) | (5) | (1) | (2) | (1) | (2) | (2) |

## HRT CONSTRUCTION

The direction of the diagonal line is crucial when cutting your starting rectangles into triangles.

Working with one set of HRTs at a time is recommended as the triangles can be difficult to track, especially when using solid fabrics!

**1.** West HRTs: Lay the following A1, B1, C1, E1 and F1 pieces tall-wise and right side facing up as shown. Cut each rectangle from bottom right to upper left and then pair the following rectangles. Refer to HRT block instructions to sew and **trim the west HRTs to 10½ x 5½in.**

**NOTE:** THE HRT CUTTING METHOD WILL YIELD AN ADDITIONAL B, C, AND F TRIANGLE THAN IS REQUIRED FOR THIS PATTERN. DISCARD OR SAVE FOR A FUTURE PROJECT!

WEST HRTS

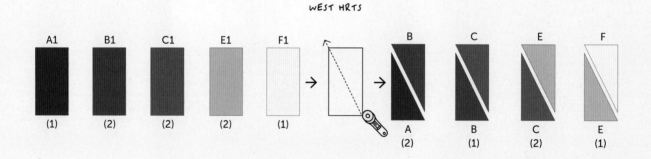

| A1 | B1 | C1 | E1 | F1 | | B | C | E | F |
| (1) | (2) | (2) | (2) | (1) | | A | B | C | E |
| | | | | | | (2) | (1) | (2) | (1) |

**2.** East HRTs: Lay the remaining A1-F1 pieces tall-wise and right side facing up as shown. Cut each rectangle from bottom left to upper right and then pair the triangles accordingly. Refer to HRT block instructions to sew and **trim the east HRTs to 10½ x 5½in.**

**NOTE:** THIS TIME, THE CUTTING METHOD WILL YIELD AN ADDITIONAL D AND E TRIANGLE TO DISCARD OR SAVE.

EAST HRTS

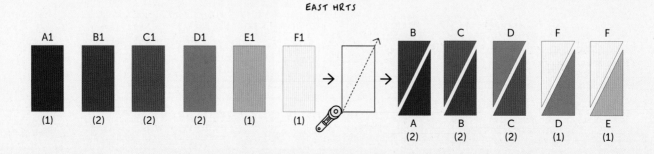

| A1 | B1 | C1 | D1 | E1 | F1 | | B | C | D | F | F |
| (1) | (2) | (2) | (2) | (1) | (1) | | A | B | C | D | E |
| | | | | | | | (2) | (2) | (2) | (1) | (1) |

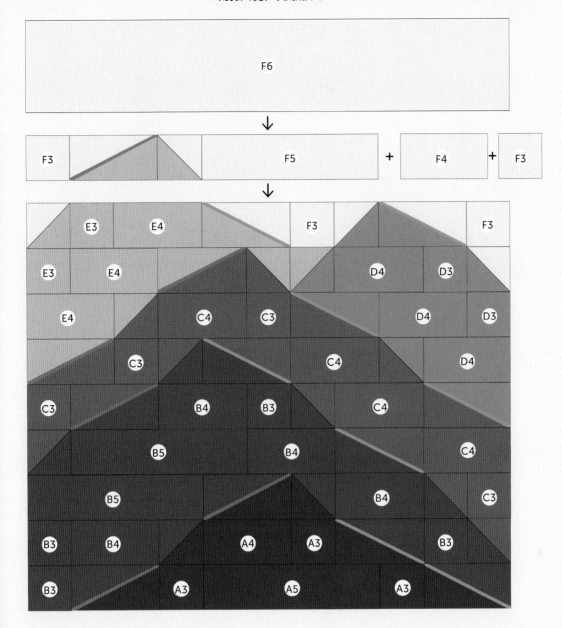

## QUILT TOP ASSEMBLY

**1.** Sew the Fabric F WOF strip and F6 along the short edge, RST, to create (1) F6 strip measuring 55½ x 10½in.

**2.** Arrange the blocks as shown in the Assembly Diagram. Ensure the HRTs and HSTs are properly oriented. West HRTs are marked orange and east HRTs are marked blue for easy tracking.

**3.** Sew the blocks into rows. Press.

**4.** Sew the rows together, pinning at each seam to keep the blocks and rows aligned. Backstitch at the start and end of each row to reinforce the seams. Press seams open.

See **Quilting + Finishing** to complete your project.

### BEHIND THE SCENES

I CREATED THIS DESIGN BEFORE I STARTED WRITING THIS BOOK SO IT'S THE FIRST LANDSCAPE OF THE BUNCH. IT'S HARD TO CHOOSE FAVORITES, BUT I AM ONE HRT-LOVING SON OF A GUN AND I AM MOST PROUD OF THIS ONE (SHHH, DON'T TELL THE OTHER DESIGNS). SINCE MY FIRST FORAY INTO HRTS YEARS AGO, I HAVE BEEN NON-STOP TRYING TO COME UP WITH WAYS TO SIMPLIFY ITS INSTRUCTIONS SO I HOPE I'VE DONE THAT HERE.

# MOUNTAIN MINIS

They say variety is the spice of life and when it comes to quilts: this is 100% true. That's why these minis were carefully planned so you can join them together to create one wide panel. Prefer to lay your head on it? Omit the top or bottom row for each panel to make a matching pillow set!

**TIP!** DON'T FORGET TO LABEL YOUR PIECES, ESPECIALLY WHEN WORKING WITH A MONOCHROMATIC COLOR SCHEME. I PERSONALLY USE PAINTER'S TAPE BECAUSE IT'S QUICK AND REUSABLE. WHEN I'M DONE, I STICK THE PIECES TO MY WALL TO SAVE FOR FUTURE USE. AS ONE DOES.

## FINISHED SIZE
20 x 25in per panel

———

## FABRIC REQUIREMENTS
(for all three panels unless noted)

| Fabric | Quantity |
| --- | --- |
| A | ⅜yd or 1 FQ |
| B | ⅝yd |
| C | ⅝yd |
| D | ⅜yd |
| E | ⅜yd |
| Backing (per panel) | ¾yd |
| Binding (per panel) | ¼yd |

———

## BASIC BLOCKS
Half rectangle triangles (HRTs)
Half square triangles (HSTs)

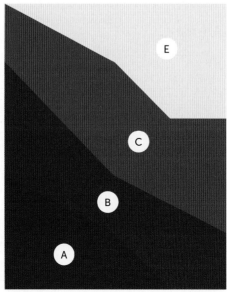

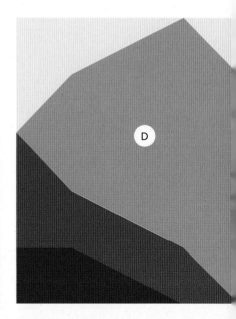

**FABRIC A**

Cut 1 piece 6in x WOF
Subcut:
(2) 12 x 6in **A1**
(1) 6in square **A2**

Cut 1 piece 5½in x WOF
Subcut:
(1) 10½ x 5½in **A4**
(1) 5½in squares **A3**

**FABRIC D**

Cut 1 piece 6in x WOF
Subcut:
(2) 12 x 6in **D1**
(2) 6in squares **D2**
(1) 5½in square **D3**

Cut 1 piece 5½in x WOF
Subcut:
(2) 15½ x 5½in **D5**

**FABRIC B**

Cut 2 pieces 6in x WOF
Subcut:
(3) 12 x 6in **B1**
(3) 6in squares **B2**
(4) 5½in squares **B3**

Cut 1 piece 5½in x WOF
Subcut:
(2) 10½ x 5½in **B4**

**FABRIC E**

Cut 1 piece 6in x WOF
Subcut:
(2) 12 x 6in **E1**
(2) 6in squares **E2**

Cut 1 piece 5½in x WOF
Subcut:
(2) 5½in squares **E3**
(1) 10½ x 5½in **E4**

# CUTTING INSTRUCTIONS

- **See Projects** for important notes before you begin.
- Skipped labels (e.g. D4) are intentional.

## BINDING FABRIC

**Cut 3 pieces**
2½in x WOF per panel

**FABRIC C**

Cut two pieces 6in x WOF
Subcut:
(3) 12 x 6in **C1**
(4) 6in squares **C2**
(3) 5½in squares **C3**

Cut 1 piece 5½in x WOF
Subcut:
(3) 10½ x 5½in **C4**

## HST CONSTRUCTION

There will be an extra C/E HST block. Discard or save for a future project.

**1.** Pair the following A2-E2 pieces, RST. Refer to HST block instructions to sew and **trim the total HSTs required to 5½in.**

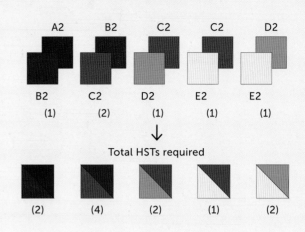

## HRT CONSTRUCTION

The direction of the diagonal line is crucial when cutting your starting rectangles into triangles.

Working with one set of HRTs at a time is recommended as the triangles can be difficult to track, especially when using solid fabrics!

**1.** West HRTs: Lay the following A1-E1 pieces tall-wise and right side facing up as shown. Cut each rectangle from bottom right to upper left and then pair the following rectangles. Refer to HRT block instructions to sew and **trim the west HRTs to 10½ x 5½in.**

NOTE: THE HRT CUTTING METHOD WILL YIELD AN ADDITIONAL A AND D TRIANGLE THAN IS REQUIRED FOR THIS PATTERN. DISCARD OR SAVE FOR A FUTURE PROJECT!

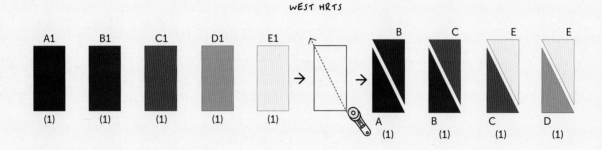

**2.** East HRTs: Lay the remaining A1-E1 pieces tall-wise and right side facing up as shown. Cut each rectangle from bottom left to upper right and then pair the triangles accordingly. Refer to HRT block instructions to sew and **trim the east HRTs to 10½ x 5½in.**

NOTE: THIS TIME, THE CUTTING METHOD WILL YIELD AN ADDITIONAL A, D, AND E TRIANGLE TO DISCARD OR SAVE.

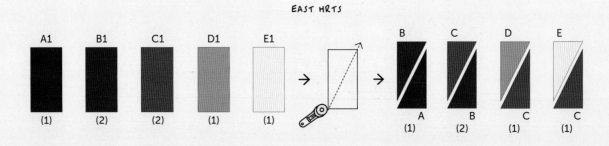

ASSEMBLY DIAGRAM: PANEL 1

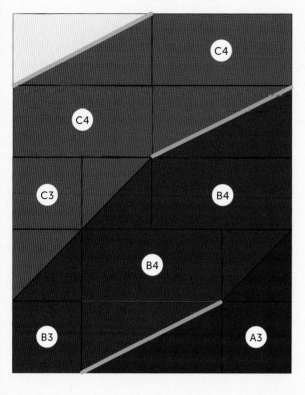

ASSEMBLY DIAGRAM: PANEL 2

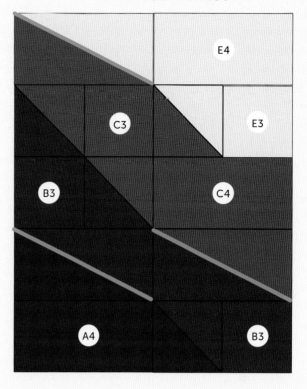

ASSEMBLY DIAGRAM: PANEL 3

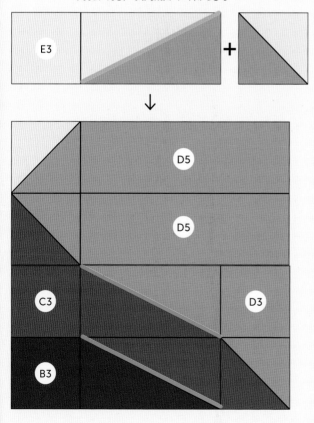

## QUILT TOP ASSEMBLY

**1.** Arrange the blocks as shown in the Assembly Diagrams. Ensure the HRTs and HSTs are properly oriented. West HRTs are marked orange and east HRTs are marked blue for easy tracking.

**2.** For each panel, sew the blocks into rows. Press.

**3.** For each panel, sew the rows together to complete the quilt tops. Press seams open.

See **Quilting + Finishing** to complete your project.

# WOODLAND

One more change of scenery for our last stop: curves. We touched on them briefly in the earlier part of our journey. This time, we're ramping it up with lots of curve-sewing to hone our skills. Let's hop out of our car, stretch our legs, and take a leisurely stroll into the woods.

## FINISHED SIZE
40 x 48in

---

## FABRIC REQUIREMENTS

| Fabric | Quantity |
| --- | --- |
| A | ⅜yd or 1 FQ* |
| B | ¼yd or 1 FQ |
| C | ⅜yd or 1 FQ |
| D | ½yd |
| E | ¼yd or 1 FQ |
| F | ⅜yd |
| G | ⅞yd |
| Backing | 2¾yds |
| Binding | ⅜yd |

*FQ is sufficient but leaves no room for error.

---

## BASIC BLOCKS
Quarter circles
Strips

---

## TEMPLATES
**See Templates** to make the convex and concave quarter circle templates

# CUTTING INSTRUCTIONS

- **See Projects** for important notes before you begin.
- Skipped labels (e.g. D2) are intentional.

**BACKING FABRIC**
**Cut 2 pieces** 48in x WOF

**BINDING FABRIC**
**Cut 5 pieces** 2½in x WOF

## FABRIC A

**Cut 2 pieces** 4½in x WOF
**Subcut:**
**(2)** 12½ x 4½in **A3**
**(2)** 8½ x 4½in **A2**
**(2)** 4½in squares **A1**
**(6)** convex pieces

**Note:** See cutting diagram if using a FQ for Fabric A.

## FABRIC B

**Cut 1 piece** 5in x WOF
**Subcut:**
**(1)** concave piece
**(3)** convex pieces
**(1)** 4½in square **B1**

## FABRIC C

**Cut 1 piece** 5in x WOF
**Subcut:**
**(4)** concave pieces
**Cut 1 piece** 4½in x WOF
**Subcut:**
**(4)** 4½in squares **C1**
**(5)** convex pieces

## FABRIC D

**Cut 3 pieces** 4½in x WOF
**Subcut:**
**(2)** 16½ x 4½in **D4**
**(1)** 4½in square **D1**
**(1)** 12½ x 4½in **D3**
**(10)** convex pieces

## FABRIC E

**Cut 1 piece** 5in x WOF
**Subcut:**
**(3)** concave pieces
**(4)** convex pieces
**(2)** 4½in squares **E1**

## FABRIC F

**Cut 1 piece** 5in x WOF
**Subcut:**
**(1)** concave piece
**(1)** 4½in square **F1**
**(1)** 12½ x 3½in **F5**
**(1)** 16½ x 3½in **F6**
**Cut 1 piece** 4½in x WOF
**Subcut:**
**(2)** 16½ x 4½in **F4**
**(2)** 4½in squares **F1**

## FABRIC G

**Cut 1 piece** 16½in x WOF
**Subcut:** see cutting diagram for clarity
**(1)** 17½ x 16½in **G6**
**(19)** concave pieces
**Cut 3 pieces** 4½in x WOF
**Subcut:**
**(1)** 32½ x 4½in **G8**
**(2)** 4½in squares **G1**
**(1)** 24½ x 4½in **G7**
**(1)** 16½ x 4½in **G4**
**(1)** 12½ x 4½in **G3**
**(2)** 8½ x 4½in **G2**
**(1)** 12½ x 1½in **G5**

FABRIC A: FQ CUTTING DIAGRAM

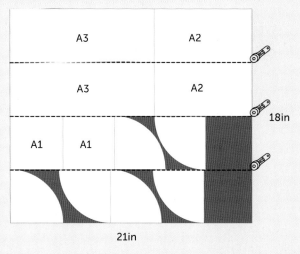

FABRIC G: CUTTING DIAGRAM

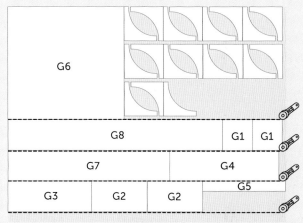

## QUARTER CIRCLE BLOCK CONSTRUCTION

**1.** Pair the following convex and concave pieces as shown. Refer to quarter circle block instructions (**see Basic Blocks**) to sew and **trim each quarter circle block to 4½in**.

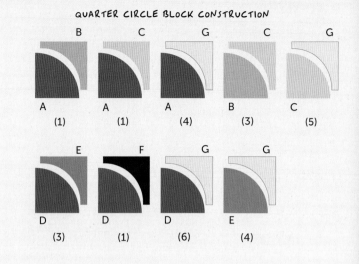

QUARTER CIRCLE BLOCK CONSTRUCTION

## TRUNK UNIT CONSTRUCTION

Refer to strip instructions (**see Basic Blocks**) for important sewing tips.

**1.** Sew the G5 piece and the F5 piece along the long edge, RST, to complete the GF5 unit. Press seams open.

**2.** Arrange the trunk blocks as shown. Sew the blocks in column 2 and column 3. Press. Sew the columns together to complete the trunk unit. Pin before sewing each column to maintain alignment. Press seams open.

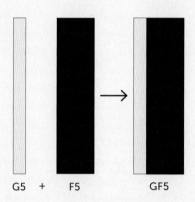

TRUNK UNIT CONSTRUCTION (STEP 1)

G5 + F5      GF5

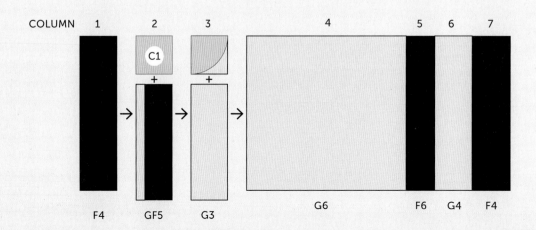

TRUNK UNIT CONSTRUCTION (STEP 2)

MATCH CURVED SEAMS

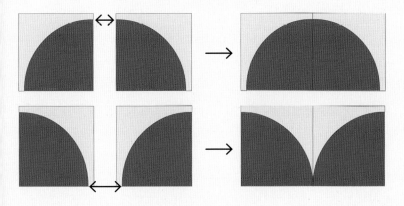

ASSEMBLY DIAGRAM

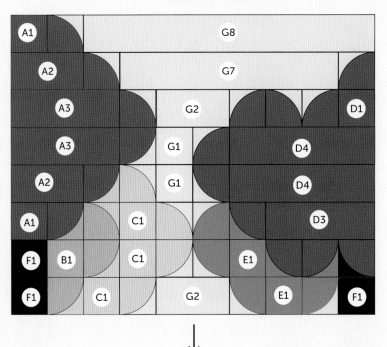

## QUILT TOP ASSEMBLY

**1.** Arrange the tree canopy blocks as shown in the Assembly Diagram. Ensure the quarter circle blocks are properly oriented. Sew the blocks into rows. Press.

---

**NOTE:** WHEN SEWING QUARTER CIRCLE BLOCKS TOGETHER, MATCH THE CURVED SEAMS AS SHOWN TO CREATE A SMOOTH AND FLUFFY TREE CANOPY.

---

**2.** Sew the rows together, pinning at each seam to keep the blocks and rows aligned. Backstitch at the start and end of each row to reinforce the seams. Press seams open.

See **Quilting + Finishing** to complete your project.

### BEHIND THE SCENES

INSECTS AND I HAVE AN UNSPOKEN AGREEMENT. I LEAVE THEM ALONE AND VICE VERSA. WHEN IT COMES TO CAMPING IN THE WOODS, ALL BETS ARE OFF. I EAT S'MORES BY THE CAMPFIRE AND THE BUGS, IN TURN, EAT ME. IT'S A VICIOUS CYCLE. ALAS, I COULDN'T LEAVE THE FOREST LANDSCAPE OUT OF THIS BOOK. HIKING IN THE WOODS MAKES ME TOO HAPPY TO CARE THAT I WILL ABSOLUTELY COME BACK HOME WITH BUG BITES.

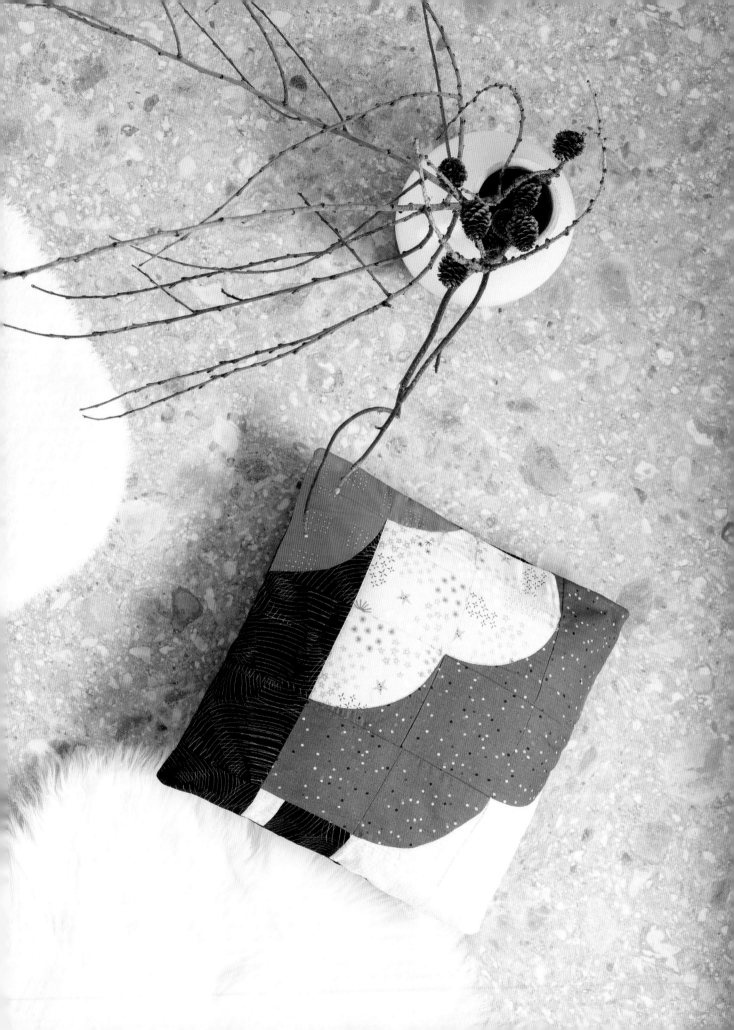

# WOODLAND MINI

So you don't want to go too deep into the woods with curves. I hear you loud and clear. Here's a quicker project to practice making quarter circle blocks. For this sample, I used wool batting to give it a poofy look. It's a petite size, making it adaptable to use for other quilty projects, such as a cute pillow. Need a little pizzazz in your dining room? Go ahead and turn it sideways for a funky placemat. You're in the driver's seat, friend.

## FINISHED SIZE
16 x 20in mini or
16 x 16in pillow

---

## FABRIC REQUIREMENTS

| Fabric | Quantity |
| --- | --- |
| A | ¼yd or 1 FE |
| B | ¼yd or 1 FE* |
| C | ¼yd or 1 FQ |
| D | ¼yd or 1 FE* |
| E | ¼yd or 1 FE* |

**For mini quilt:**

| | |
| --- | --- |
| Backing | ⅝yd |
| Binding | ¼yd |

**For pillow:**

| | |
| --- | --- |
| Backing | ⅜yd |

*FE is sufficient but leaves no room for error

---

## BASIC BLOCK
Quarter circles

---

## TEMPLATES
**See Templates** to make the convex and concave quarter circle templates

# CUTTING INSTRUCTIONS

- **See Projects** for important notes before you begin.
- Refer to concave and convex cutting instructions (**see Basic Blocks**) for directions on how to cut the fabrics using templates.

## PILLOW BACKING FABRIC

**Cut 1 piece** 12¼in x WOF
**Subcut:**
**(2)** 16½ x 12¼in

## MINI QUILT BINDING FABRIC

**Cut 3 pieces** 2½in x WOF

### FABRIC A

**Cut 1 piece** 4½in x WOF
**Subcut:**
**(1)** 4½in square **A1**
**(2)** convex pieces

### FABRIC B

**Cut 1 piece** 5in x WOF
**Subcut:**
**(1)** concave piece
**(3)** convex pieces
**(1)** 4½in square **B1**

**Note:** See cutting diagram if using a FE for Fabric B.

### FABRIC C

**Cut 1 piece** 5in x WOF
**Subcut:**
**(3)** concave pieces
**(2)** convex pieces
**(4)** 4½in squares **C1**

### FABRIC D

**Cut 1 piece** 5in x WOF
**Subcut:**
**(1)** concave piece
**(3)** 4½in squares **D1**
**(1)** 3½ x 4½in **D2**

**Note:** See cutting diagram if using a FE for Fabric D.

### FABRIC E

**Cut 1 piece** 5in x WOF
**Subcut:**
**(2)** concave pieces
**(3)** 4½in squares **E1**
**(1)** 1½ x 4½in **E2**

**Note:** See cutting diagram if using a FE for Fabric E.

FABRIC B: FE CUTTING DIAGRAM

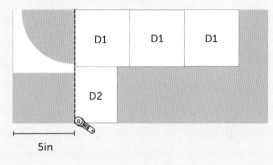

B1

5in

FABRIC D: FE CUTTING DIAGRAM

D1    D1    D1

D2

5in

FABRIC E: FE CUTTING DIAGRAM

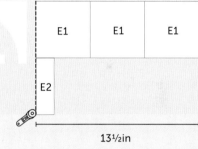

E1    E1    E1

E2

13½in

## QUARTER CIRCLE BLOCK CONSTRUCTION

**1.** Pair the following convex and concave pieces as shown. Refer to quarter circle block instructions (**see Basic Blocks**) to sew and **trim each quarter circle block to 4½in.**

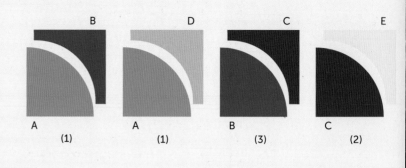

QUARTER CIRCLE BLOCK CONSTRUCTION

B · D · C · E

A (1) · A (1) · B (3) · C (2)

## TRUNK UNIT CONSTRUCTION

**1.** Sew the D2 piece and the E2 piece along the long edge, RST, to complete the ED2 unit. Press seams open.

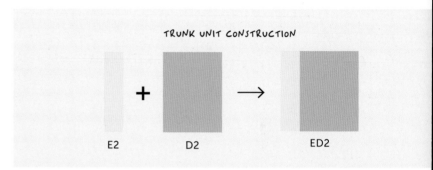

TRUNK UNIT CONSTRUCTION

E2 **+** D2 → ED2

## QUILT TOP ASSEMBLY

**1.** Arrange the blocks as shown in the Assembly Diagram. Ensure the quarter circle blocks are properly oriented. Sew the blocks into rows. Press.

---

**NOTE**: WHEN SEWING QUARTER CIRCLE BLOCKS TOGETHER, MATCH THE CURVED SEAMS TO CREATE A SMOOTH AND FLUFFY TREE CANOPY.

---

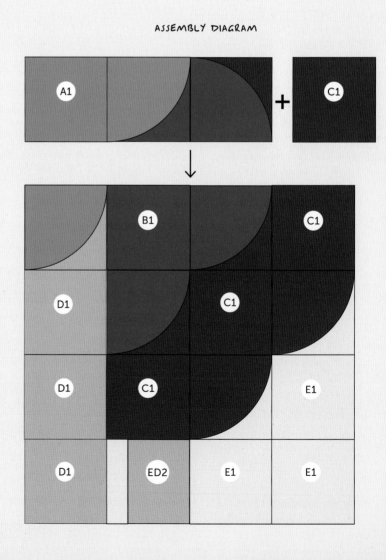

ASSEMBLY DIAGRAM

MAKING THE PILLOW

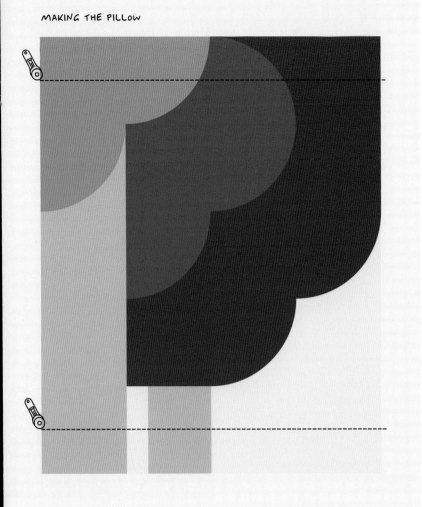

**2.** Sew the rows together to complete the quilt top, pinning at each seam to keep the blocks and rows aligned. Press seams open.

If making the pillow, trim 2in off the top and bottom of your quilt top to create a 16½in square.

See **Quilting + Finishing** to complete your project.

# QUILTING + FINISHING

After your quilt top is assembled, it's time to baste, quilt, and finish your creation. I enjoy using different methods to complete my projects, so it was important for me to make sure that you have the same options. That said, the following pages include an overview on how to quilt by machine or by hand.

You'll also find a choice of step-by-step instructions to finish your project. Whether you prefer to face your quilt versus traditionally binding it, sew by hand versus machine, or make a wall hanging versus a pillow, I was determined to make this book thorough and versatile. Because of all the possible different routes, I would suggest reading through the instructions to see which method works best for you before you make a selection. Remember to take plenty of breaks and stretch those muscles!

# TOOLS FOR QUILTING

Once your quilt top is pieced, the following are other recommended tools, including a separate list to complete your project by machine or by hand.

## GENERAL TOOLS

**1** **Batting.** I used Warm & White cotton batting for most of the projects in the book. Try wool batting for a puffier look (check out the Woodland Mini project for a sample).

**2** **Hera marker.** Nifty tool for marking your quilting guidelines on the fabric.

**3** **Curved Safety Pins** or **Fabric Adhesive Spray.** To temporarily hold the three layers of a quilt together (**see Quilt sandwich**).

**4** **Quilting Clips.** Great for temporarily holding your quilt edges or binding fabric in place.

## QUILTING BY MACHINE

**5** **Quilting gloves.** The special fingertip coating on these gloves helps you control the layers of fabric through the sewing machine.

**6** **Walking Foot.** A specialty foot for stitching a quilt together more evenly and with more precision. This may or may not have come with your sewing machine so please refer to your sewing machine manual.

## QUILTING BY HAND

**7** **Needle threader.** Handy tool for inserting thread through the eye of the needle.

**8** **Thimble(s).** A guard to prevent fingertips from discomfort when pushing your embroidery needle through layers.

**9** **Thread.** A thicker thread than that used for machine quilting is recommended to withstand the force of pulling and stretching. The thickness is also a great size for showing off your deserve-to-be-seen hand stitches. I typically use 8-weight thread for my projects.

**10** **Embroidery Needle.** These come in different sizes (the lower the number, the bigger the needle). Choosing the right size for you depends on your comfort level and your thread weight. I typically use milliner needles in size 7 or 9.

# QUILT SANDWICH

Now that you have a completed quilt top, give it a good pressing to flatten your seams. In addition, remove and snip off loose threads on the back. Before you start quilting, the layers need to be held together temporarily, a process known as basting or making a quilt sandwich (yum!).

## THE BACKING (BOTTOM LAYER)

Backing fabric should be larger than your quilt top to account for fabric shifting during the quilting process. For the main projects, the backing fabric yardage requirements include an extra 4in on all sides. Mini projects (except for Lake) include an extra 3in on all sides.

Trim off the backing fabric selvages and press to remove wrinkles and unwanted folds. If the cutting instructions of a project require more than one piece of backing fabric, it will need to be pieced together. Use a ½in inch seam allowance to join the pieces and press your seams open to reduce bulk.

## THE BATTING (MIDDLE LAYER)

There are different types of batting depending on:

- loft (thickness)
- size (comes pre-packaged or on the bolt)
- fiber content (cotton, cotton/poly blends, wool, polyester, bamboo, etc.)

Most of the projects in this book used Warm & White cotton batting. I find it reliable, sturdy, and it does not stretch as easily as others. On the other hand, wool batting was used for the Canyon, Mountain (purple), Woodland Mini, and Canyon Mini (no sun) projects. The loft of wool batting often provides a puffier quilt and showcases the quilt stitches beautifully.

### BATTING SCRAPS

If you have lots of batting leftover from previous projects, try piecing your batting scraps together for a no-waste alternative. For this method, you simply put two pieces of leftover batting side by side, with straight edges touching, and use the zigzag stitch of your sewing machine to join them together.

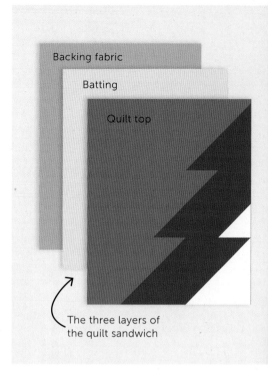

The three layers of the quilt sandwich

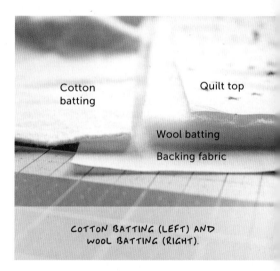

COTTON BATTING (LEFT) AND WOOL BATTING (RIGHT).

## LONGARM QUILTING

If you're sending your quilt top to a longarmer — a magical person who takes care of the basting and quilting for you — refer to their backing and quilt top preparation requirements. For more info on longarming, **see Machine Quilting**.

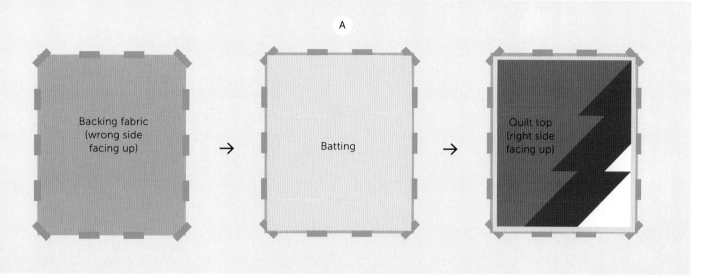

A

Backing fabric (wrong side facing up) → Batting → Quilt top (right side facing up)

B

USE A RULER WITH YOUR HERA MARKER TO HELP YOU PLAN AND MARK GUIDELINES FOR QUILTING.

C

CURVED SAFETY PINS MAKE IT CONVENIENT TO SCOOP ALL THREE LAYERS WITH EASE.

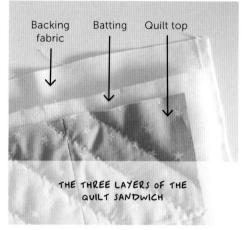

Backing fabric    Batting    Quilt top

THE THREE LAYERS OF THE QUILT SANDWICH

## BASTING YOUR QUILT

The following instructions are based on my go-to method – pin basting – because it's reusable and inexpensive.

### PIN BASTING

**1.** With the wrong side facing up, lay your backing fabric on a hard surface that's large enough to spread your entire quilt. Ensure the fabric is smooth and flat, then secure to the surface generously with painter's tape **(A)**. Make sure the backing fabric is not loose or overstretched.

**2.** Place your batting on top. Smooth the batting from the center to the edges to flatten out bubbles and creases. Be careful not to shift the backing underneath.

**3.** Center your quilt top (right side up) on top of the batting, once again smoothing the layer from the center to the edges to eliminate bubbles and creases.

**4.** If you have a quilt design in mind, mark where your quilting stitches will go with a Hera marker **(B)**.

**5.** Starting from the center of the quilt, use safety pins to secure the three layers together. Continue to pin, spacing them at about 4in apart from each other **(C)**. To quilt your project, **see Quilting**.

Remember to mark your quilting guidelines *before* you pin, as I forgot to do here **(B)**! The safety pins can make it tricky to mark your quilt design.

SPRAY BASTING: ANOTHER WAY OF BASTING IS TO USE FABRIC ADHESIVE SPRAY. THIS TENDS TO BE EASY AND FAST, BUT HAS A BIGGER ENVIRONMENTAL IMPACT. IF YOU DECIDE TO USE FABRIC ADHESIVE SPRAY TO BASTE YOUR QUILT, THE FOLLOWING QUILTING INSTRUCTIONS ARE ALMOST IDENTICAL TO THOSE FOR PIN BASTING. JUST REMEMBER TO FOLLOW THE MANUFACTURER'S INSTRUCTIONS, APPLYING THE ADHESIVE BETWEEN EACH LAYER AND PRESSING THE BASTED QUILT AFTERWARD.

# QUILTING

It's time to make your three layers into an official quilt by stitching them together! Quilting not only holds your three layers in place, but it can also dramatically add depth and visual interest to your project.

A simple quilt design, such as straight lines, provides a modern look that tends to let the project design shine. More complex quilting patterns, such as echoing the angles of the project design, can add dimension to your quilt. You can also mix both – add simple quilting to the background, while going fancy on a particular section to accentuate certain landscape features.

Take time to plan out your quilt design – or not! Improvisation can be an effective method to express your creativity and allow your imagination to run wild.

Once you've finished quilting, **see Squaring Up**.

## CREATIVE TRICKS

Don't forget to tap into your adventurous side when quilting! Consider the following:

- Change thread colors
- Vary thread weight
- Combine hand and machine quilting

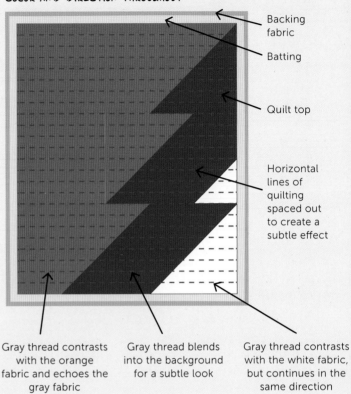

QUILTING USING THE SAME THREAD COLOR AND DIRECTION THROUGHOUT

Backing fabric

Batting

Quilt top

Horizontal lines of quilting spaced out to create a subtle effect

Gray thread contrasts with the orange fabric and echoes the gray fabric

Gray thread blends into the background for a subtle look

Gray thread contrasts with the white fabric, but continues in the same direction

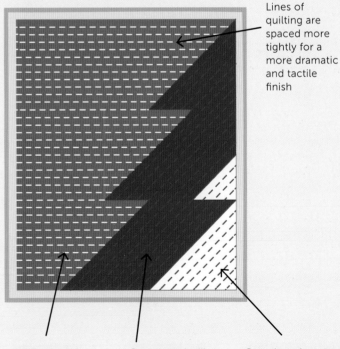

THE THREAD COLOR AND DIRECTION VARIED TO ACCENTUATE THE DESIGN

Lines of quilting are spaced more tightly for a more dramatic and tactile finish

White thread contrasts with the orange and picks up on the white in the fabric color palette

Gray thread still blends into the background, but echoes the design with subtle texture

Gray thread contrasts with the white, while the direction again echoes the design

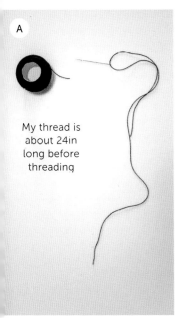

My thread is about 24in long before threading

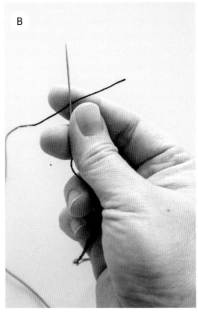

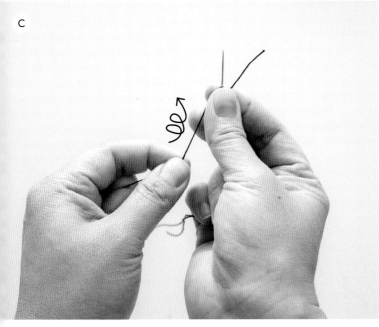

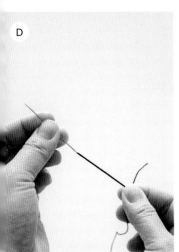

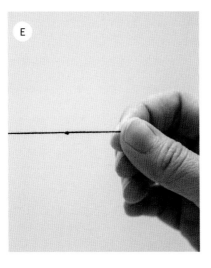

## HAND QUILTING

Here's a confession: it took me several years to learn to love hand quilting. It requires patience because it can be very time-consuming, but I've also come to realize how therapeutic and comforting it can be. It's auditory and tactile, making the process subtly stimulating and soothing at the same time.

Many hand quilters use a quilting hoop to keep their layers taut as they stitch. I prefer to use a table and my free hand to help guide the layers to the hand that's holding the needle. I use 8-weight thread: the thickness withstands the tugging, while the silky texture enhances the look and feel of your finished quilt. Personally, if I'm going to be spending a lot of time quilting, the stitches better be visible!

### 1. PREPARING THE NEEDLE AND THREAD

Begin by threading your needle – my thread is about 24in long **(A)**. Then, tie a quilter's knot. To do so, place the end of the thread perpendicular to the needle and pinch with your thumb and forefinger **(B)**. Wind the thread around the needle twice (for 12-weight or thicker) or three times (for thinner threads). Pull the remainder downward **(C)**. Slowly pull the needle away with your free hand, keeping your pinched thumb and forefinger together as they move along with the wound thread **(D)**. When you are 1–2in from the end of the thread, release your fingers and pull the knot taut **(E)**.

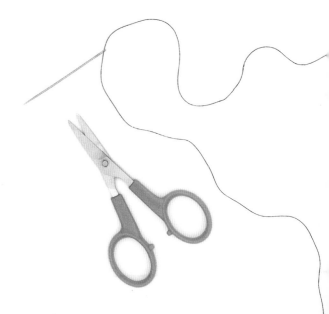

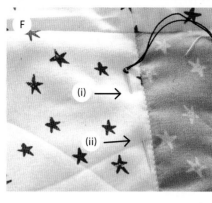

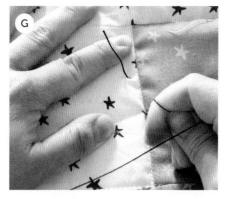

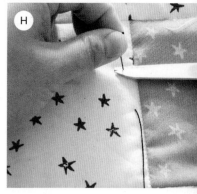

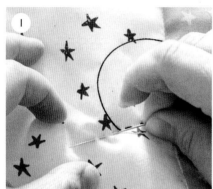

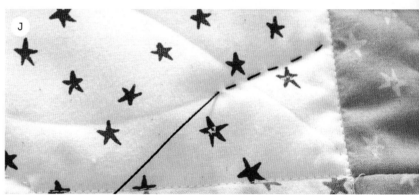

### 2. ANCHORING YOUR THREAD

Locate a point about 2in away from where you want to make your first stitch **(F)**. From this point, take your needle through the first and second layers of the quilt (the top and batting only) **(i)** then go back up to the point where you will make your first stitch **(ii)**. As you pull the needle through, your knot will land on the surface of your quilt top. Tug your thread until you hear a "pop" and see the knot disappear underneath **(G)**.

Snip the tail end if it's still visible **(H)**. If you notice a tiny hole made from the knot puncturing your woven fabric, give that area a gentle rub until the hole is no longer noticeable.

### 3. STARTING TO STITCH

Stitch through all three layers (quilt top, batting, and backing), following your marked guidelines (if any), and readjusting the quilt as you go to prevent the layers from bunching up. Use your non-dominant hand to help guide and weave the needle through the layers **(I)**. Note that the length of your stitches may vary **(J)**.

---

**FINDING YOUR FLOW STATE:** IT MAY TAKE SOME MORE PRACTICE TO FIND YOUR RHYTHM, BUT ONCE YOU DO, YOU MAY FIND THE REPETITIVENESS TO BE MEDITATIVE AND COMFORTING.

---

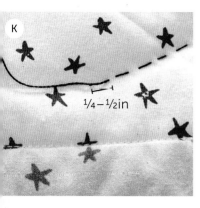

¼–½in

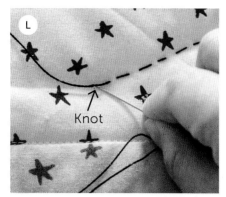

Knot

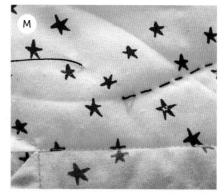

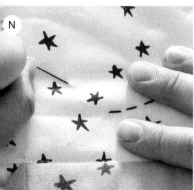

## 4. CHANGING YOUR THREAD

When your thread is starting to feel too short to continue, it's time to change your thread. First, tie a regular knot, leaving a ¼–½in gap between the knot and surface of the quilt **(K)**. Make the final puncture within the ¼in gap between the knot and the quilt surface. Otherwise, the knot will remain on the surface **(L)**. Then, take your needle through the first and second layers of your quilt – again, do not go through the backing fabric.

Bring the needle back up about 2in from your last stitch, and away from your stitching path **(M)**. Tug your thread until you hear a "pop" and see your knot disappear **(N)**. Snip the end of your thread and give that area a slight rub until the thread end disappears **(O)**.

Repeat steps 1–4 until you're finished quilting.

## MACHINE QUILTING

Machine quilting is the faster method for quilting. Also, the stitches are smaller, and typically neater than those created by hand. However, wrestling three layers of fabric through your home sewing machine can be quite a workout!

### WHERE TO START?

When I am machine quilting, I tend to choose straight-line quilting for my projects. I roll up my quilt halfway, and quilt from the middle out. This allows the quilt's weight to be distributed more evenly on either side of my arms. It also pushes any fabric "bubbling" during this process to the fabric edges. Depending on your quilt design, you may need to try different positions to find your comfort level before proceeding.

### PREPARING YOUR SETUP

I find it helpful to place a second table behind my sewing table. This supports my quilt as it feeds through the machine, making the process less cumbersome **(A)**. My gloved hands **(see Tools For Quilting)** are positioned on either side of the walking foot to guide the quilt through the machine **(B)**. This hand position helps to keep the layers flat, preventing unwanted puckers and folds.

### HOW TO CHANGE DIRECTION

If you need to change direction, first keep your needle in the down position to keep the quilt in place. Lift your walking foot and gently rotate the quilt in your desired direction. With the needle still down, lower the walking foot and resume quilting.

### TAKE YOUR TIME

As tempting as it is to put the pedal to the metal, try to resist speeding through this process. It has the tendency to show up on your quilt, leading to undesirable results.

---

*STAY STRONG:* REMEMBER TO TAKE PLENTY OF BREAKS. A PROLONGED QUILTING POSITION IS A RECIPE FOR SORE NECK AND SHOULDER MUSCLES.

---

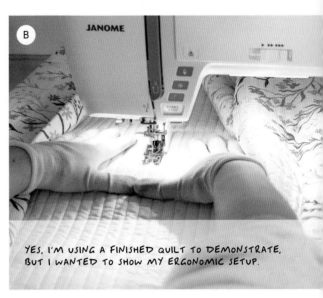

YES, I'M USING A FINISHED QUILT TO DEMONSTRATE, BUT I WANTED TO SHOW MY ERGONOMIC SETUP.

## LONGARM QUILTING

Longarm quilting is arguably the fastest but most expensive method for quilting your project. A longarm quilting machine is both bulky and costly, but it skips the entire basting process because the three layers of your quilt are rolled and loaded onto a rack to be stitched. The needle moves to the desired area, rather than the quilt being moved to the stationary needle of a home sewing machine. This allows a lot more versatility to achieve intricate quilt designs.

Due to the high investment of owning a longarm machine, there are many professional longarm quilters who offer quilting services for a fee. The talented contributors who quilted the main projects in this book are listed in the **Resources** section.

### PREPARE FOR HANDOVER

If you are sending your quilt to a longarm quilter, refer to their preparation requirements for your backing and quilt top.

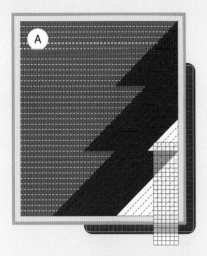

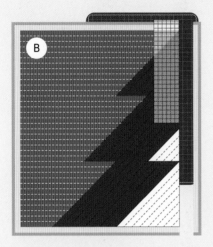

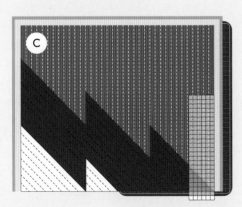

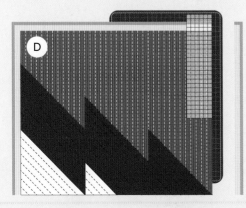

# SQUARING UP

Before you bind your quilt, you need to trim off the excess batting and backing fabric to ensure your quilt is squared up. In other words, you are making the quilt edges straight and all corners a 90-degree angle. To do this, we'll start with the bottom right corner of your quilt:

**1.** Place your quilt flat on the floor, ideally on a surface large enough to spread out the entire quilt. (Otherwise, roll up the left half of the quilt, ensuring the right half is smooth and flat.) Tuck your cutting mat underneath the trimming area.

**2.** Align the edge of your ruler on the edge of your quilt top. Align one of the pieced horizontal seams of your quilt with one of the horizontal marks on your ruler. Trim the excess batting and backing fabric as far as the length of the ruler allows **(A)**.

**3.** Without moving your quilt, slide the ruler and cutting mat up to the next part of the quilt top. To do this, align the newly trimmed edge and one of the horizontal quilt seams with the horizontal marks on your ruler, and trim. Continue this way until you've completed trimming one side of the quilt **(B)**.

**4.** Move your cutting mat to lie beneath the next side to be trimmed. (If the quilt has been half-rolled, readjust the roll as well.) To align the edge of your ruler on this second edge, align the newly trimmed side of the quilt with the horizontal marks on your ruler **(C)**. Trim the excess batting and backing fabric. Repeat step 3 as necessary **(D)**.

**5.** Repeat step 4 for the two remaining sides.

## QUILT TOP TOO SHORT OR NARROW?

Some areas of your quilt top may extend past the edge of your ruler. For the projects in this book, it's fine to include these slim areas as you square up your quilt.

On the other hand, some areas of your quilt top might not even reach the edge of your ruler:

- If the edge of the quilt top **is** comfortably within the ¼in seam allowance, only trim the batting and backing fabric of that area – the binding will hide that minor issue.

- If the edge of the quilt top **is not** comfortably within the ¼in seam allowance, consider re-trimming that entire side to accommodate this too-short quilt top area. You can also adjust the binding seam allowance to ensure you catch the area as you sew the binding to the front of the quilt.

# FINISHING A QUILT

We're on the home stretch, my friend! The final step to complete your quilt is covering the raw edges. Traditional binding is the standard method, creating a classic, definitive frame. You can bind the strips to the back of the quilt by machine or hand – I'll show you how to do both.

*NOTE:* THE SEAM ALLOWANCE IS ¼IN THROUGHOUT, UNLESS OTHERWISE NOTED.

## METHOD 1: TRADITIONAL BINDING

While the project cutting instructions are based on the standard 2½in width to make your binding strips (allowing room for error), a 2¼in width is also a popular choice. Feel free to adjust the width of your strips at this point. This narrower width can create a snug fit when you attach the binding to the back of the quilt, which may be more desirable to you.

### JOINING BINDING STRIPS

**1.** Shorten your stitch length to 2.0 on your sewing machine to reinforce your seams. Place two binding strips perpendicularly at the ends, RST, as shown on the diagram. Mark a diagonal line from corner to corner, where the ends overlap **(A)**. Sew a diagonal seam on the marked line **(B)**. Repeat until all strips are pieced together into one long binding strip.

**2.** Trim excess fabric ¼in away from each seam **(C)**. Press the seams open and remove dog ears.

**3.** With WST, press the strip in half along its entire length **(D)**.

### ATTACHING BINDING TO THE FRONT

Use your sewing machine to attach the first side of the binding to the front of the quilt.

**1.** Leaving the first 6in of the strip unsewn, sew the binding to the front of the quilt along one of the sides (away from the corners), aligning the raw edges of the binding to the raw edges of the quilt. Stop and backstitch ¼in away from the corner's edge **(E)**.

**2.** Remove the quilt from the machine and rotate it 90-degrees counterclockwise. Flip the binding up, away from the quilt to create a diagonal fold **(F)**. Note that the 45-degree angle of the fold hits the corner of the quilt.

**3.** Flip the binding down, toward the quilt, to create a second fold along the top edge of the quilt **(G)**.

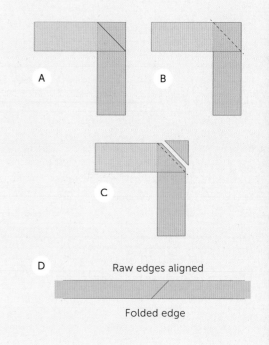

Raw edges aligned

Folded edge

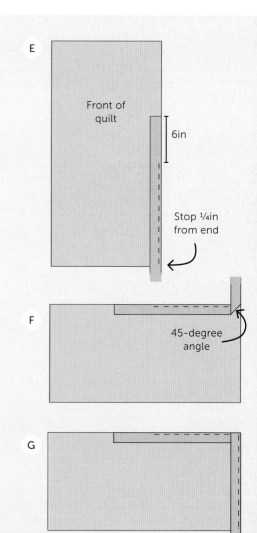

Front of quilt

6in

Stop ¼in from end

45-degree angle

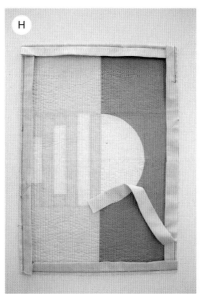

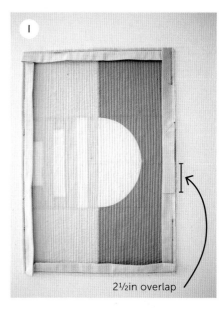

2½in overlap

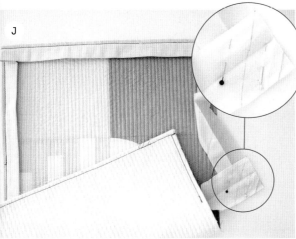

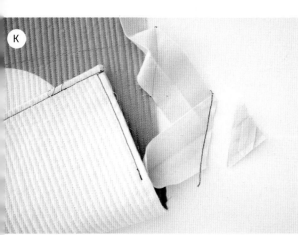

**4.** Resume sewing the binding to the front of the quilt, repeating steps 2 and 3 for the remaining corners. Stop and backstitch about 12in away from where you first attached the binding. You will likely have a tail of binding that will be longer than you need, but do not cut it yet!

**5.** Straighten your quilt so the quilt edge where the strip ends need to be joined is resting nice and flat on a surface. Place the top tail (which may be longer than shown on the diagram) on top of the bottom tail, keeping the raw edges aligned **(H)**. Trim the top tail so the ends only overlap by 2½in (or 2¼in if you opted for a narrower binding strip) **(I)**.

**Note:** The overlap is equal to the width of your unfolded binding strip.

**6.** Unfold the ends and position them RST so that the bottom tail (with its right side facing down) is on top of the top tail (with its right side facing up). In order for the ends to meet, you'll need to either bunch up the quilt a bit or fold the quilt up from the bottom to give the binding some slack **(J)**.

**7.** Secure the ends with pins and mark a diagonal line from corner to corner. Sew a diagonal seam on the marked line to join the binding strip. Trim excess fabric ¼in away **(K)**. Press the seam open and remove dog ears.

**8.** Fold the newly joined strip in half, WST. Complete sewing the binding to the front of the quilt, backstitching at the start and end to secure the seam.

### PREPARING TO ATTACH BINDING TO THE BACK

Start securing the binding to the back of the quilt with quilting clips **(L)**. The folded edge should extend over the seam allowance. As you secure the binding, it will somewhat create a natural diagonal fold when you get to a corner **(M)**. Finger press to emphasize this fold, then continue securing with binding clips to create crisp, mitered corners.

Back of quilt:
¼in seam allowance →

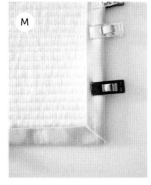

KEEP GOING: DON'T BE DETERRED BY THE LENGTH OF THESE INSTRUCTIONS. THE PROCESS IS EASIER DONE THAN SAID, SO LET'S FINISH STRONG!

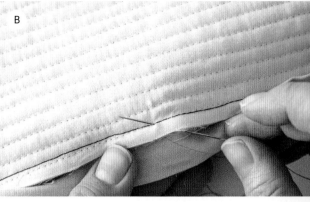

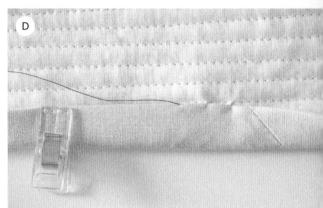

## ATTACHING BINDING TO THE BACK: BY HAND

The following hand sewing method is called invisible stitching. 50- or 40-weight cotton thread is the standard, as it will hide the stitches better than thicker thread. In addition, choose a thread color that matches the binding fabric (I'm using dark thread for demonstration only).

**Pro:** Invisible stitches are used to create a clean look on both sides of the quilt.

**Con:** This is the slowest option and, depending on skill level, may not feel as secure as machine binding.

---

**FOR MY FELLOW LEFT-HANDED QUILTERS:**
THE HAND BINDING DIAGRAMS ARE BASED
ON A RIGHT-HANDED PERSPECTIVE.

---

**1.** With about 20in of thread, thread the needle and tie a double or triple knot at one end. I wrap the single thread around my finger a couple of times and roll it out with my thumb to create a knot. Don't worry if the knot isn't tidy. **(A)**.

**2.** Starting from within the seam allowance, take your needle through the backing fabric and come up through the ¼in seam allowance **(B)**. My untidy knotted end will remain hidden within the ¼ seam allowance **(C)**. Continue your needle through the folded edge of the binding (or from the previous stitch, if you're repeating this step) **(D)**.

**3.** Next to the previous stitch, take your needle through about ¼in of the backing fabric towards the left and bring it back up through the folded edge of the binding **(E)**.

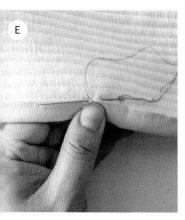

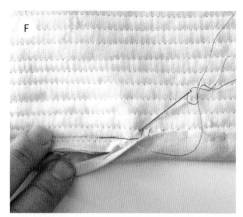

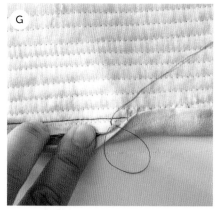

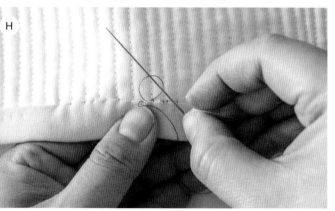

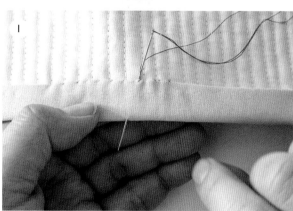

**4.** Repeat step 3 until your thread is starting to feel short and difficult to manage. **Important:** As shown in **(E)**, use your non-dominant hand to keep the binding tight and firmly secured to the quilt while sewing.

**5.** When your thread is starting to feel short and cumbersome: next to the previous stitch, take the needle through the backing fabric, towards the raw edge of the quilt **(F)**. Note: Ideally, you're not pulling down the binding and unraveling the stitches, like I'm doing here. This is only for a visual aid!

**6.** Take the needle through a tiny piece of backing fabric and as you go up, take your needle through the loop it created to make a knot **(G)**. Snip the end of your thread.

**7.** Repeat steps 1–6 as needed until you've sewn around the perimeter of the quilt.

**8.** When you've reached the end, continue a few stitches past the first stitch. Then, take your needle to grab a tiny piece of backing fabric (next to the last stitch). As you go up, take your needle through the loop that it created to make a knot **(H)**. Next to the knot, take your needle through the binding fabric and out to the edge of the quilt **(I)**. Snip the end of your thread. Now, take a bow, do a jig, or cuddle under your new quilt. Your quilt is finished!

## ATTACHING BINDING TO THE BACK: BY MACHINE

### OPTION 1: FRONT OF QUILT

With the quilt front facing up, slowly stitch-in-the-ditch (a method of sewing on an existing seam) along the binding. When you reach the beginning, backstitch to reinforce the stitches.

**Pro:** The stitches will not be noticeably visible from the front **(A)**.

**Con:** Since the folded edge of the binding strip is on the back of the quilt, it will be trickier to finish attaching the binding to the quilt. Moreover, the binding strip (from the back of the quilt) may not look as neat **(B)**.

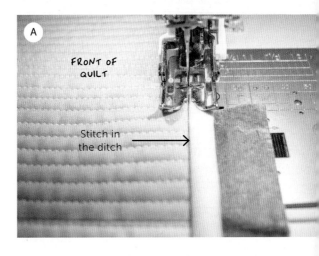

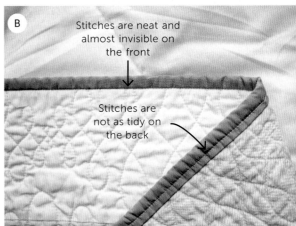

### OPTION 2: BACK OF QUILT

With the quilt back facing up, slowly sew by the folded edge of the binding strip.

**Pro:** It's faster and easier. The binding strip (from the back of the quilt) will look neat and clean **(C)**.

**Con:** Your stitches will be visible on the front, which may leave an undesirable result **(D)**.

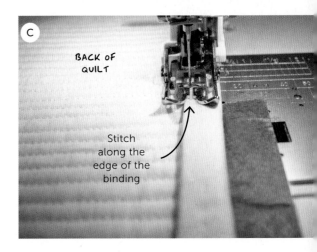

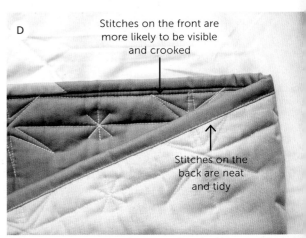

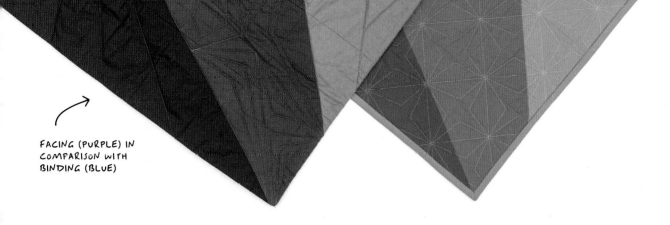

FACING (PURPLE) IN
COMPARISON WITH
BINDING (BLUE)

## METHOD 2: QUILT FACING

For a minimal, clean look, I often gravitate towards quilt facing: a finishing method that folds the entire width of the binding strip onto the back of the quilt. This allows the landscape design to shine. With this option, you will be hand binding the strips to the back of the quilt.

### SEWING THE QUILT FACING

We'll focus on a technique that may not result in the flattest corners and edges, but I use this one the most because it's the quickest and fastest way to face a quilt!

**1.** Sew binding strips (if needed) along the short edge, RST, until you create a total of (2) strips that are the same width as your quilt. With WST, press each strip in half along the length.

**2.** Align the raw edges of each strip to the raw edges of the top and bottom sides of the quilt front. Secure with quilting clips and sew to the front of the quilt **(A)**.

**3.** Sew binding strips (if needed) along the short edge, RST, until you create a total of (2) strips that are the same height as your quilt. Press each strip in half along the length, WST. Then, trim off ½in from each strip.

**4.** Center each strip to the front sides of the quilt, raw edges aligned. The strip is ½in shorter than the height, which means there will be a ¼in gap from the corners. Secure with quilting clips and sew to the quilt **(B)**.

**5.** Clip the corners to remove the excess bulk, being careful not to trim where the seams meet **(C)**.

**6.** Flip the facing strips, including the bulky seam allowance, to the back of the quilt. Press to flatten the bulk and secure the edges with quilting clips.

**See Wall Hangings + Pillows** to add corner tabs. Otherwise, **see Finishing a Quilt** to attach the binding to the back by hand.

A

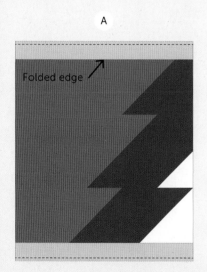

Folded edge

B

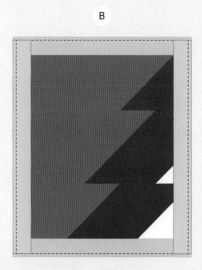

C

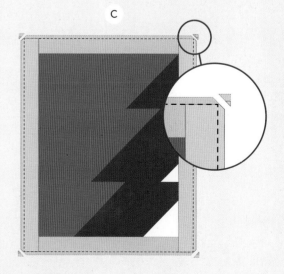

# WALL HANGINGS + PILLOWS

Prefer to hang your mini quilt on a wall or to rest your head on it for some beauty sleep? I've got you covered! The following instructions are suitable for all the mini projects, except for Lake Mini, due to its weight and size.

## MAKING A WALL HANGING

These quick corner tabs allow you to insert a wooden dowel into the back of smaller mini-quilts to create an instant wall hanging. Once you've created the corner tabs, make sure to place them on the top two corners of the back of your quilt – and under the binding. If they're placed in other corners of the quilt, you may be inadvertently preparing the quilt to hang sideways or upside down. Is this an oddly specific warning because this happened to me? Who can say...

---

### WALL-HANGING PROJECTS:

- Canyon Mini
- Coastal Mini
- River Mini
- Meadow Mini
- Mountain Minis
- Woodland Mini

---

**1.** Measure the quilt's width and divide it by three to determine the approximate square size.

**Example:** If the quilt is 20 x 25in, cut two pieces of fabric each measuring 6½in square (20 ÷ 3 = approx. 6½in).

**2.** Cut two squares, then fold along the diagonal, WST **(A)**. Press.

**3.** Tuck the corner tabs under the binding, with the raw edges aligning with the top two corners of the back of the quilt **(B)**. Secure with binding clips and basting pins, if needed, so the tabs are nice and taut (loose, saggy corners might make it tricky to level your wall hanging!).

**See Finishing a Quilt** to attach the binding to the back of the quilt by machine or by hand.

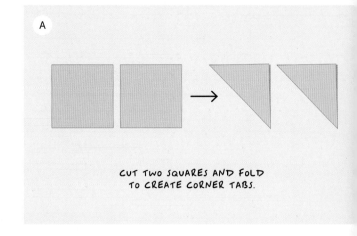

A

CUT TWO SQUARES AND FOLD
TO CREATE CORNER TABS.

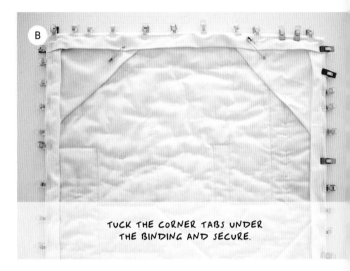

B

TUCK THE CORNER TABS UNDER
THE BINDING AND SECURE.

CUT A LENGTH OF DOWEL TO FIT
NEATLY BETWEEN THE CORNERS.

Wrong side
of panel

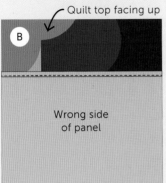

Quilt top facing up

Wrong side
of panel

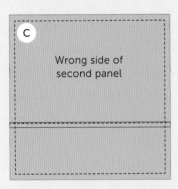

Wrong side of
second panel

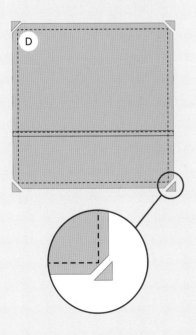

## MAKING A PILLOW

Envelope pillow covers, where the back has overlapping panels that are not sewn shut, are my favorite kind because, yep, you've guessed it – it's fast and easy. Best of all, without a zipper enclosure, these are less likely to leave a mark on your face after a friendly pillow fight.

---

### PILLOW BACKING SIZE

In the projects, the backing fabric panels are already calculated in the cutting instructions. However, the following backing panel formula allows you adapt other projects to make a pillow:

Measure the quilt top's height and divide by two. Then, add 4in. The width of each panel will be the same width as your quilt top.

**Example:** If the quilt top is a 20½in square: (20½in ÷ 2) + 4in = 14¼in. The two backing fabric panels will each measure 20½ x 14¼in.

---

**1.** Make about a ⅜in fold on one of the long sides of a panel, WST. Press. Fold again to encase the raw edge and press. Sew on top of the fold, close to the folded edge to secure it **(A)**. Repeat with the other panel to create a total of (2) panels.

**2.** Place one panel on the quilted top, RST, with the folded edge at the center **(B)**. Place the other panel on top, wrong side up, so that the folded edges overlap **(C)**. Secure with quilting clips.

**3.** Sew around the perimeter with a ½in seam allowance, backstitching on the folded edges to reinforce them. Clip the corners to remove the bulky corners, being careful not to trim where the seams meet **(D)**.

---

*SEWN FOR STRENGTH: BACKSTITCHING AND A ½IN SEAM ALLOWANCE ARE RECOMMENDED TO WITHSTAND A PILLOW COVER'S HARD LIFE OF BEING THROWN, PULLED, AND TUGGED.*

---

**4.** Turn the cover inside out and poke the corners with a pointy, but dull object. Insert the pillow form and place your head on it. Take a well-deserved nap because you are done!

---

*PLUMP IT UP: USE A PILLOW INSERT THAT IS 1-2IN LARGER THAN THE FINISHED PILLOW COVER TO CREATE A FULLER LOOK. FOR INSTANCE, IF YOUR PILLOW COVER IS 20 x 20IN, CHOOSE A 22 x 22IN PILLOW INSERT.*

# GLOSSARY

To get you up to speed on quilt lingo, below are common terms and abbreviations you'll encounter in this book (and in most quilt patterns).

**Backstitch.** Sewing 1–2 stitches backward and forward to prevent the end of a seam from unraveling.

**Baste/basting.** The process of preparing your layers for quilting by temporarily holding them together using pins or a fabric adhesive spray. Also known as making a quilt sandwich.

**Chain piecing.** A time-saving technique of sewing multiple blocks, like an assembly line, without breaking the thread.

**Dog ears.** Tiny triangles that stick out when triangles such as HST, HRT, and equilateral triangles are sewn and pressed.

**Directional fabrics.** Printed fabrics that need to be sewn in a certain direction. The projects in this book assume your fabrics are non-directional.

**FE.** Fat Eighth. A precut fabric measuring 21 x 9in.

**Finger press.** Pressing with your fingers.

**Finished size.** The size of a completed quilt after its edges have been sewn into a quilt. No raw edges are exposed. Note: The dimensions listed in each project are the finished sizes.

**FQ.** Fat Quarter. A precut fabric measuring 21 x 18in.

**HRT.** Half Rectangle Triangle. A basic quilt block.

**HST.** Half Square Triangle. A basic quilt block.

**Nesting seams.** When the seams of two blocks are pressed in opposite directions so their seams will lock into place.

**Non-directional fabrics.** Fabrics that can be sewn in any direction.

**Pre-wash.** Washing your fabrics before starting a project (**see Understanding Fabrics**).

**Quilt assembly.** When the blocks and pieces of a quilt top are ready to be sewn together.

**RST.** Right Sides Together. The front (or printed) sides of two fabric pieces face each other.

**Scant ¼in seam.** Seam allowance is a thread width narrower than ¼in to account for fabric loss after the seam is pressed (**see Basic Blocks**).

**Seam allowance.** The area between the fabric edge and the stitching/seam line. The standard is ¼in. However, a scant ¼in seam allowance is recommended to make the basic blocks in this book.

**Selvage.** The self-finished edge of a woven fabric (**see Understanding Fabrics**).

**Strip piecing.** A time-saving technique where long strips of fabric are sewn together and then subcut into smaller pieces.

**Subcut.** Cutting an already cut piece of fabric into smaller pieces (**see Pressing + Cutting**).

**Unfinished size.** The size of a quilt top or quilt block with its raw edges still exposed.

**WOF.** Width of fabric.

**WST.** Wrong Sides Together. The back (or non-printed) sides of two fabric pieces face each other.

**Yardage.** The project's fabric length requirements. The fabric requirements in this book are calculated in yards , but see the Fabric Shopping Conversion Chart for measurements in meters if that's how you buy your fabric..

# TEMPLATES

Templates are actual size. Trace onto regular paper, then transfer onto heavier cardstock or cardboard to create stability while cutting your fabrics.

- Triangle height is based on its center:

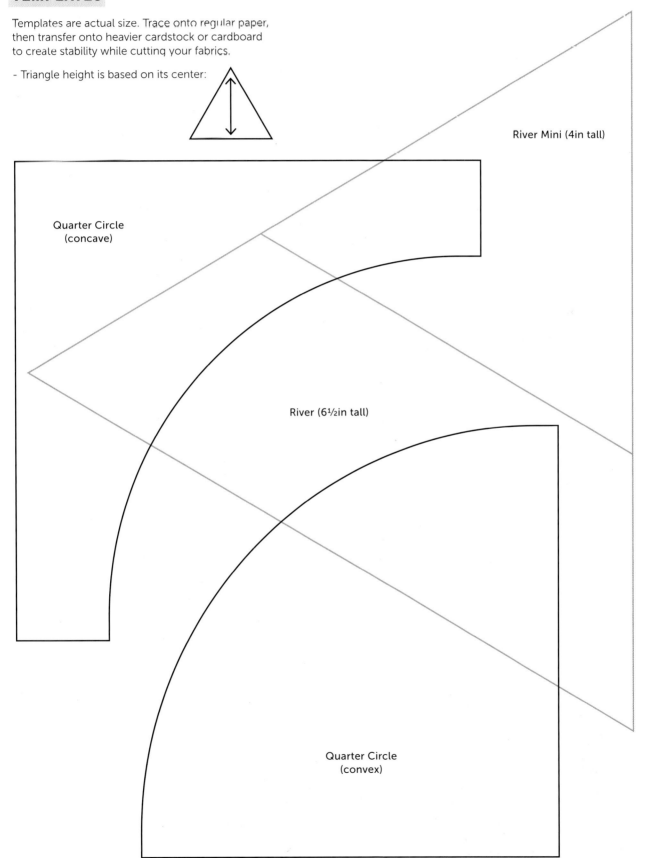

River Mini (4in tall)

Quarter Circle
(concave)

River (6½in tall)

Quarter Circle
(convex)

# RESOURCES

## FABRICS

Solid top and backing fabrics in this book were generously provided by:

**Moda Fabrics + Supplies**
*(Bella Solids)*
www.modafabrics.com

**Michael Miller Fabrics**
*(Cotton Couture)*
www.michaelmillerfabrics.com

**Robert Kaufman Fabrics**
*(Kona cotton, Essex Yarn Dyed and Brussels Washer)*
www.robertkaufman.com

**Art Gallery Fabrics** *(PURE Solids)*
www.artgalleryfabrics.com

The fabric names are compiled below for easy reference.

Printed fabrics (backing excluded) were from my stash, but their names can be found at **www.xoxsew.com**.

### 01 Lake *(Robert Kaufman)*

**A** Ice Frappe
**B** Jungle
**C** Chartreuse
**D** Graphite
**E** Overcast
**F** Quicksilver
**G** Natural
**Backing** AFRX-14469-12 Widescreen Grey

### 02 Lake Mini solids version *(Robert Kaufman)*

**A** Brussels Washer Pink Clay
**B** Essex Yarn Dyed Charcoal
**C** Essex Yarn Dyed Lingerie
**Backing** #E024-1143 Flax Wide

### 03 Lake Mini prints version *(personal stash)*

### 04 Canyon *(Art Gallery)*

**A** Sienna Brick
**B** Toasty Walnut
**C** Georgia Peach
**D** Marmalade
**E** Coconut Milk
**F** Snow
**Backing** Wide-10201 Hillside Meadow

### 05 Canyon Minis *(personal stash)*

### 06 Coastal *(Moda)*

**A** Sea
**B** Marine
**C** Storm
**D** Melon
**E** Cantaloupe
**F** Eggshell
**G** White Bleached
**Backing** #RS4051-11 108in Moonglow Natural

### 07 Coastal Mini *(Moda)*

**A** Charcoal
**B** Saffron
**C** Snow

### 08 River *(personal stash)*

### 09 River Mini *(Robert Kaufman)*

**A** Fog
**B** Oasis
**C** Mushroom
**D** Cobblestone
**E** Oyster
**Backing** #E024-1143 Flax Wide

### 10 Meadow *(Art Gallery)*

**A** Sprout
**B** Snow
**C** Dark Citron
**D** Golden Bronze
**E** Fresh Sage
**F** Asparagus
**G** Eucalyptus
**H** Latte
**J** Vanilla Custard
**K** Macchiato
**Backing** Wide-10201 Hillside Meadow

### 11 Meadow Mini *(Robert Kaufman)*

**A** Essex Yarn Dyed Metallic Water
**B** Kona Snow
**C** Brussels Washer Pink Clay
**D** Kona Earth
**E** Essex Yarn Dyed Charcoal

### 12 Mountain in purple *(Michael Miller)*

**A** Plum
**B** Eggplant
**C** Venus
**D** Mauve
**E** Iris
**F** Moon
**Backing** #WBX6774-Gray-D Vine Maze Wideback

### 13 Mountain in blue *(Moda)*

**A** Harbor
**B** Imperial Blue
**C** Bright Sky
**D** Little Boy Blue
**E** Surf
**F** Pastel Blue
**Backing** #RS11171 13 108in What Not Blue Ribbon

### 14 Mountain Mini *(Moda)*

**A** Barn Door
**B** Pomegranate
**C** Shocking Pink
**D** Fuchsia
**E** Amelia Pink

### 15 Woodland *(Robert Kaufman)*

**A** Terracotta
**B** Ochre
**C** Daffodil
**D** Roasted Pecan
**E** Yarrow
**F** Coffee
**G** Natural
**Backing** #AFRX-14469-294 Widescreen Yarrow

### 16 Woodland Mini solids version *(Michael Miller)*

**A** Electric
**B** Peacock
**C** Cobalt
**D** Wind
**E** Ice Blue

### 17 Woodland Mini prints version *(personal stash)*

## BATTING

**The Warm Company**
*(Warm & White Batting)*
www.warmcompany.com

## LONGARM QUILTING

**Trace Creek Quilting (US)**
www.tracecreekquilting.com
*(Edge-to-edge and binding services for Lake, Coastal, River, Meadow, Mountain in Blue, and Woodland projects)*

**Wild Phil Quilting (US)**
www.wildphilquilting.com
*(Custom quilting and binding services for Mountain in Purple and Canyon projects)*

# FABRIC SHOPPING CONVERSION CHART

Imperial measurements are used throughout the book. If you prefer to use metric for shopping, please use this chart. (Conversions are approximate.)

Divide yard value by 1.094 for conversions not listed below.

| Yards (yd) | Meters (m) |
|:---:|:---:|
| ⅛ | 0.15 |
| ¼ | 0.25 |
| ⅜ | 0.35 |
| ½ | 0.50 |
| ⅝ | 0.60 |
| ¾ | 0.70 |
| ⅞ | 0.80 |
| 1 | 0.95 |
| 1⅛ | 1.1 |
| 1¼ | 1.2 |
| 1⅜ | 1.3 |
| 1½ | 1.4 |
| 1⅝ | 1.5 |
| 1¾ | 1.65 |
| 1⅞ | 1.8 |
| 2 | 1.9 |

## TECHNICAL PATTERN EDITING

**Village Bound Quilts**
www.villageboundquilts.com

**Sarah Ruiz Quilts**
www.saroy.net

# ABOUT THE AUTHOR

Donna McLeod is the modern quilter and pattern designer behind XOXSEW. She was introduced to quilting at the tender age of thirty-something, and fell in love with this forgiving, therapeutic craft. With a fondness for simplicity, Donna is steadfast about writing instructions and making video tutorials that are clear and concise. When not in her sewing room, she enjoys hiking (reluctantly), reading books and playing video games (avidly), and spending time with her family (almost always).

For more patterns and tutorials, please visit **www.xoxsew.com**.

# ACKNOWLEDGMENTS

**Matt**, your constant encouragement to find my personal joy is a big reason this book happened. Thank you for being my rock every day and somehow knowing exactly what I needed throughout this process without my asking. Also, don't forget that your wife thanked you here first and foremost.

A giant quilt-sized hug to my girls. You both inspire me every day to go out of my comfort zone and to embrace the simplicities in life. If you're reading this: Hi, I-love-you-goodnight-sweet-dreams!

Special thanks to **Sarah Callard**, for reaching out and handing me an opportunity to turn my childhood fantasy of writing a book into reality. **Jen Fox-Proverbs**: thank you for your editing expertise and reassuring emails. Also, an enormous thanks to everyone at *David & Charles*: **Jess Cropper, Anne Williams, Anna Wade, Jess Pearson, Lucy Ridley, Lee-May Lim**, and **Jeni Chown**, for all your hard-working contributions. **Brandon Conklin**, thanks for not only taking photos amidst weather extremes, but for taking great care of my quilts in the wild.

A debt of gratitude to **Lilo Whitener-Fey**, for always being game to collaborate with me. You make it easy to reach out to you and I'm so grateful for your support. Many thanks to **Mindy Mounteer** for your custom work.

**Tiffany Horn**, you went above and beyond for the book and helped ease my anxiety from start to finish. Thank you for tech editing and everything in between. Also, to **Sarah Ruiz**, for your helpful suggestions and feedback.

To the generous folks at *Art Gallery Fabrics, Michael Miller Fabrics, Moda Fabrics*, and *Robert Kaufman Fabrics*: I had the best time playing with your fabrics. Thank you for providing the fabrics that became the quilts in the book. Many thanks to **Lindsey** of *The Warm Company*, for supplying my go-to batting.

**Wendy Chow**: thank you for your words of encouragement, guidance, and for putting up with my I-have-no-idea-what-I'm-doing texts. **Heather L.**, thank you for giving me the proper tools to keep my mental health in check. I can't see you without employer-based healthcare coverage, but there's absolutely no way I would ever thank an insurance company.

A hearty thanks to my quilty pals: **Alissa Strouse, Alyssa Sheldon, Pam Leen**, and **Daphné Parthoens**. Your time and energy for testing some of the projects in the book did not go unnoticed. You're all a gem and I'm grateful for your support and friendship.

Thank you to the online quilt community and to everyone who has cheered me on since the start of **XOXSEW** and my quilt journey. You keep me going, even when my tank is empty.

And finally, to you. There's a ton of fantastic quilt projects out there, so it means the world to me to have this book in your lovely, capable hands.

# INDEX

Publishing Director: Ame Verso
Senior Commissioning Editor: Sarah Callard
Managing Editor: Jeni Chown
Editor: Jessica Cropper
Project Editor: Jenny Fox-Proverbs
Technical Editor: Anne Williams
Head of Design: Anna Wade
Designers: Anna Wade + Lee-May Lim
Pre-press Designer: Sue Reansbury
Art Direction: Laura Woussen, Jess Pearson + Lucy Ridley
Photography: Brandon Conklin + Jason Jenkins
Production Manager: Beverley Richardson

David and Charles publishes high-quality books on a wide range of
subjects. For more information visit www.davidandcharles.com.

Share your makes with us on social media using #dandcbooks and
follow us on Facebook and Instagram by searching for @dandcbooks.

The contents of the book were written with print books in
mind. Layout of the digital edition of this book may vary
depending on reader hardware and display settings.